The Magic of the Mind

An Exposition of the Kālakārāma Sutta

by

Bhikkhu K. Ñāṇananda

Buddhist Publication Society
Kandy • Sri Lanka

Buddhist Publication Society
P.O. Box 61
54, Sangharaja Mawatha
Kandy, Sri Lanka

First published in 1974
Reprinted 1985, 1997, 2011

National Library and Documentation Centre -
Cataloguing-in-Publication (CIP) Data

Nyanananda himi, K.
Magic of the Mind: An exposition of the Kālakārāma Sutta / K. Nyanananda himi: - Kandy : Buddhist Publication Society Inc., 2011
BP 405 S. - 106p.: 22cm

ISBN 955-24-0135-6

i. 294.3823 DDC 22
1. Tripitaka 2. Sutrapitaka

ISBN 955-24-0135-6

Typeset at the BPS in URW Palladio Pali

Printed by
Samayawardana Printers,
Colombo 10.

About the Author

Bhikkhu Ñāṇananda is a Buddhist monk of Sri Lanka. Before his ordination he was an assistant lecturer in Pali at the University of Peradeniya. After entering the Buddhist Order in 1969 he has resided mostly in remote hermitages. Currently he is living at Potgulgala Araññā near Kegalla. His other publications by the BPS are:

Concept and Reality in Early Buddhist Thought (BP No. 404)

Saṃyutta Nikāya Anthology: Part II (Wheel No. 183/185)

Ideal Solitude (Wheel No. 188)

Contents

Etadatthā, bhikkhave, kathā, etadatthā mantanā, etadatthā upanisā, etadatthaṃ sotāvadhānam, yadidaṃ anupādācittassa vimokkho.

Conversation, monks, is for this purpose, consultation is for this purpose, reliance is for this purpose, lending-ear is for this purpose, that is to say, for the clinging-free deliverance of the mind.

(A I 198).

List of Abbreviations

A	Aṅguttara Nikāya
A-a	Aṅguttara Commentary
D	Dīgha Nikāya
D-a	Dīgha Nikāya Commentary
Dhp	Dhammapada
Dhp-a	Dhammapada Commentary
DPP	*Dictionary of Pali Proper Names*
It	Itivuttaka
M	Majjhima Nikāya
PTS	Pali Text Society (ed).
S	Saṃyutta Nikāya
S-a	Saṃyutta Nikāya Commentary
SHB	Simon Hewavitaraṇa Bequest (ed.)
Sn	Suttanipāta
Th	Theragāthā
Ud	Udāna
Vin	Vinaya Piṭaka

Introduction

Kāḷakārāma Sutta—Historical Background

The Kāḷakārāma Sutta was preached by the Buddha to the monks while he was staying at the Kāḷaka monastery in Sāketā. Apart from mention of the venue, the discourse, as it is recorded in the Aṅguttara Nikāya (II 24ff.), is not placed in any significant context to show us how it was inspired. The commentary (A-a 34) finds for it a setting in the aftermath of the conversion of the millionaire Kāḷaka, who is supposed to have constructed the monastery. According to it, the discourse was a sequel to the widespread acclamation of the Buddha's marvellous qualities. Be that as it may, the discourse, as a matter of fact, does contain some marvellous aspects of the Tathāgata's transcendental wisdom. That the impact of the discourse was actually astounding is symbolically expressed by the commentarial assertion that the earth trembled at five points in this sermon, at the conclusion of which five hundred monks attained Arahantship.

The Sutta gains a high degree of historical importance owing to the tradition handed down by the commentaries and chronicles,[1] that it was preached by the venerable Mahārakkhita Thera to convert the country of the Yonakas during the great missionary movement which took place in the reign of the Emperor Asoka. If the identification of the Yonakas with Greeks is correct, the choice of this deeply philosophical discourse for such a significant occasion, could not have been a mere coincidence. It might have been prompted by the consideration that the philosophically mature minds of the Greeks would be able to receive it well. Tradition has it that the impact of the discourse on the

1 See DPP I 573 f.

Yonakas was considerable, for thirty-seven thousand people attained to the Fruits of the Path on hearing it (op. cit.).

The Buddhists of ancient Ceylon, too, seem to have recognized the value of the Kāḷakārāma Sutta as a theme capable of mustering the essence of Dhamma for a lengthy sermon. One memorable occasion on which it formed the subject of an all-night sermon was when the arahant Kāḷa ("Black") Buddharakkhita Thera preached it on the dark night of the new-moon day of the dark fortnight under a black Timbaru tree at Cetiyapabbata. The coincidence of "darkness" (*kāḷa*) in the names of the Sutta and the preacher as well as in the environment probably accounts for the memorability of the occasion. The presence of King Tissa (probably Saddhātissa) in the audience may also have contributed its share of dignity to the occasion.

Significance of the Sutta

In spite of its hallowed tradition, today, at any rate, the *Kāḷakārāma Sutta* can hardly be regarded as popular. It rarely comes up as a subject of a sermon and allusions to it in serious expositions of the Dhamma are equally rare. This, however, is no index to its degree of relevance to modern times. The "darkness" of near-obscurity in which the Sutta finds itself today is probably due to its terseness and its resemblance to the unfamiliar tetralemma.[2] To the superficial reader the Sutta presents a mosaic of dry phrases and a set of statements that go against the grain. But beneath that dryness and that strangeness in formulation there lie vast resources for a perennial philosophy. The Sutta brings out some striking features of the epistemology of early Buddhism, the implications of which would go a long way in clearing up the

2. Sanskrit: *catuṣkoṭi* the Buddhist logic of four alternatives (affirmative, negative, both affirmative and negative, neither … nor). See the text of the Sutta (ed.).

muddle that exists in the fields of philosophical and psychological research even in this modern age.

Mode of Presentation

In order to prepare the mind of the reader for a proper appreciation of the *Kāḷakārāma Sutta*, Chapter I will treat him to a "magic-show," which will serve as a prologue to the exposition attempted in the present work. The "magic-show," however, is by no means a profane element here, since it is merely an amplification of a canonical prototype attributed to the Buddha himself. Beginning with the canonical simile proper, the prologue will expand into a kind of parable which—though a trifle modern in its flavour—is designed to "lubricate" the reader's mind in view of the "dry" discourse that will follow. In a limited sense, it will also serve as a framework for discussion.

Chapter II will present the translation of the Sutta followed by a few explanatory notes, some of which are from venerable Buddhaghosa's commentary to the Sutta. The purpose of these notes is to see that some sense emerges out of the text as it stands, with many variant readings. A deeper appreciation of the actual contents of the Sutta will, however, be reserved for the subsequent chapters.

The simile and the parable given in Chapter I will attempt to prove their worth in the nine chapters that follow, the last of which forms the Epilogue. The illusory nature of consciousness will be discussed in the contexts of the doctrinal categories known as *khandha* (aggregates), *āyatana* (spheres), *dhātu* (elements) and *paṭicca-samuppāda* (Dependent Arising). These chapters will regularly draw upon the "well-preached Dhamma-word" (*dhammapadaṃ sudesitaṃ*) scattered throughout the Suttas, putting them together—as far as possible—into a garland of flowers.[3] All along, similes and analogies, both canonical and modern, will

3. The allusion is to vv 44, 45 of the Dhp.

illustrate the relevant facts, for, "even with the help of a simile some intelligent men here comprehend the meaning of what is said.[4]"

Bhikkhu Ñāṇananda
Island Hermitage
Dodanduwa, Sri Lanka
October, 1972

4. See D II 324, M I 384.

CHAPTER I

The Magic-Show—A Prologue

"... Suppose, monks, a magician or a magician's apprentice should hold a magic-show at the four cross-roads; and a keen-sighted man should see it, ponder over it and reflect on it radically.[5] Even as he sees it, ponders over it and reflects on it radically, he would find it empty; he would find it hollow; he would find it void of essence. What essence, monks, could there be in a magic show?

Even so, monks, whatever consciousness—be it past, future or present, in oneself or external, gross or subtle, inferior or superior, far or near—a monk sees it, ponders over it and reflects on it radically. And even as he sees it, ponders over it and reflects on it radically, he would find it empty; he would find it hollow; he would find it void of essence. What essence, monks, could there be in a consciousness? ..."[6]

Form is like a mass of foam
And feeling but an airy bubble.
Perception is like a mirage
And formations a plantain tree.
Consciousness is a magic-show,
A juggler's trick entire.
All these similes were made known
By the "Kinsman-of-the-Sun."[7] (S III 142)

---

5. I.e., *yoniso manasikāra*—lit: "reflection by way of source or matrix."

6. Cf. "Impermanent, O monks, are sense-pleasures; they are hollow, false and delusive; they are conjuror's tricks, O monks, tricks which make the fools prattle." (M II 261, *Āneñjasappāya Sutta*).

7. *Ādiccabandhu*: an epithet of the Buddha.

The famous magician whose miraculous performances you have thoroughly enjoyed on many an occasion, is back again in your town. The news of his arrival has spread far and wide, and eager crowds are now making for the large hall where he is due to perform today. You too buy a ticket and manage to enter the hall. There is already a scramble for seats, but you are not keen on securing one, for today you have entered with a different purpose in mind. You have had a bright idea to outwit the magician—to play a trick on him yourself. So you cut your way through the thronging crowds and stealthily creep into some concealed corner of the stage.

The magician enters the stage through the dark curtains, clad in his pitch black suit. Black boxes containing his secret stock-in-trade are also now on the stage. The performance starts and from your point of vantage you watch. And as you watch with sharp eyes every movement of the magician, you now begin to discover, one after the other, the secrets behind those "breathtaking" miracles of your favourite magician. The hidden holes and false bottoms in his magic boxes, the counterfeits and secret pockets, the hidden strings and buttons that are pulled and pressed under the cover of the frantic waving of his magic-wand. Very soon you see *through* his bag of wily tricks so well that you are able to discover his next "surprise" well in advance. Since you can now anticipate his "surprises," they no longer surprise you. His "tricks" no longer deceive you. His "magic" has lost its magic for you. It no longer kindles your imagination as it used to do in the past. The magician's "hocus-pocus" and "abracadabra" and his magic-wand now suggest nothing to you—for you know them now for what they are, that is: "meaningless." The whole affair has now turned out to be an empty show, one vast hoax—a treachery.

In utter disgust, you turn away from it to take a peep at the audience below. And what a sight! A sea of craned necks—eyes that gaze in blind admiration; mouths that gape in dumb appreciation; the "Ah!"'s and "Oh!"'s and whistles of speechless amazement. Truly, a strange admixture of tragedy and comedy which you could have enjoyed instead of the magic-show, if not for the fact that you yourself were in that same sorry plight on many a previous occasion. Moved by compassion for this frenzied crowd, you almost frown on the magician as he chuckles with a sinister grin at every applause from his admirers. "How is it," you wonder, "that I have been deceived so long by this crook of a magician?" You are fed up with all this and swear to yourself—"Never will I waste my time and money on such empty shows, *nev-ver.*"

The show ends. Crowds are now making for the exit. You too slip out of your hiding place unseen and mingle with them. Once outside, you spot a friend of yours whom you know as a keen admirer of this magician. Not wishing to embarrass him with news of your unusual experience, you try to avoid him, but you are too late. Soon you find yourself listening to a vivid commentary on the magic performance. Your friend is now reliving those moments of the "bliss-of-ignorance" which he had just been enjoying. But before long he discovers that you are mild and reserved today, and wonders how you could be so, after such a marvellous show.

> "Why? You were in the same hall all this time, weren't you?"
> "Yes, I was."
> "Then, were you sleeping?"
> "Oh! No."
> "You weren't watching closely, I suppose."
> "No, no, I was watching it alright, may be I was watching too closely."
> "You say you were watching, but you don't seem to have seen the show."
> "No, I saw it. In fact I saw it so well that I missed the show!"

CHAPTER II

Kāḷakārāma Sutta

At one time the Exalted One was staying at Sāketā in Kāḷaka's monastery. There the Exalted One addressed the monks, saying: "Monks." "Revered Sir," replied those monks in assent. The Exalted One said:

"Monks, whatsoever in the world with its gods, Māras and Brahmas, among the progeny consisting of recluses and brahmins, gods and men—whatsoever is seen, heard, sensed,[8] cognized, attained, sought after and pondered over by the mind—all that do I know. Monks, whatsoever in the world ... of gods and men—whatsoever is seen ... by the mind—that have I fully understood; all that is known to the Tathāgata,[9] but the Tathāgata has not taken his stand upon it.[10]

"If I were to say: 'Monks, whatsoever in the world ... of ... gods and men—whatsoever is seen ... by the mind—all

---

8. *Muta*: sensations arising from taste, touch and smell.

9. According to the Commentary (A-a): "the plane of omniscience" (*sabbaññutā-bhūmi*) has been made known by the three phrases: "all that do I know," "that have I fully understood" and "all that is known to the Tathāgata."

10. Commentary: "The Tathāgata does not take his stand upon, or approach by way of craving or views. The Exalted One sees a form with the eye, but in him there is no desire and lust (for it); he is well released in mind. The Exalted One hears a sound with the ear ... smells an odour with the nose ... tastes a flavour with the tongue ... touches a tangible with the body ... cognizes an idea with the mind, but in him there is no desire-and-lust; he is well released in mind (S IV 164)—hence was it said that the Tathāgata takes no stand upon it. It should be understood that by this phrase the plane of the influx-free (*khīṇāsava-bhūmi*) is made known."

that I do not know'—it would be a falsehood in me.[11] If I were to say: 'I both know it and know it not'—that too would be a falsehood in me. If I were to say: 'I neither know it nor am ignorant of it'—it would be a fault in me.[12]

"Thus, monks, a Tathāgata does not conceive[13] of a visible thing as apart from sight;[14] he does not conceive of an unseen;[15] he does not conceive of a 'thing-worth-seeing';[16] he does not conceive about a seer.[17]

"He does not conceive of an audible thing as apart from hearing; he does not conceive of an unheard; he does not conceive of a 'thing-worth-hearing'; he does not conceive about a hearer.

"He does not conceive of a thing to be sensed as apart from sensation; he does not conceive of an unsensed; he does not conceive of a 'thing-worth-sensing'; he does not conceive about one who senses.

---

11. This rendering is in accordance with the reading *na jānāmi* found in the Chaṭṭha Saṅgīti edition. Enquiries have revealed that it conforms to the Mandalay Slabs. The PTS edition, as well as some Sinhala script editions, gives *jānāmi*, omitting the negative particle, but this is unlikely, as it contradicts the Buddha's own statement in the preceding paragraph. The initial declaration "all that do I know" (*tamahaṃ jānāmi*) is reinforced by what follows: "that have I fully understood" (*tamahaṃ abbhaññāsiṃ*), "all that is known to the Tathāgata (*taṃ tathāgatassa viditaṃ*). A significant reservation has also been added: "but the Tathāgata has not taken his stand upon it" (*taṃ tathāgato na upaṭṭhāsi*). Hence the reading *jānāmi* would lead to a contradiction: "If I were to say … all that do I know… it would be a falsehood in me." The variant reading *"na jānāmi,"* on the other hand, suggests itself as the second alternative of the tetralemma, followed as it is by the third and fourth alternatives. The relevance of these three alternatives to the context is reflected in that reservation referred to above.

12. The phrases: "it would be a falsehood in me," "that too would be a falsehood in me," "it would be a fault in me," are said to indicate the "plane of truth" (*sacca-bhūmi*).

"He does not conceive of a cognizable thing as apart from cognition; he does not conceive of an uncognized; he does not conceive of a 'thing-worth-cognizing;' he does not conceive about one who cognizes.

"Thus, monks, the Tathāgata being such-like in regard to all phenomena seen, heard, sensed, and cognized, is 'such.' Moreover, than he who is 'such,' there is none other greater or more excellent, I declare. [18]

Whatever is seen, heard, sensed or clung to,
is esteemed as truth by other folk,
Midst those who are entrenched in their own views,[19]
being "such" I hold none as true or false.

---

13. *Na maññati*: *Maññanā* marks that stage in sense perception when one egotistically imagines or fancies a perceived "thing" to be out there in its own right. It is a fissure in the perceptual situation which results in a subject-object dichotomy perpetuating the conceit: "I" and "mine."

14. The Commentary (A-a SHB 519) takes the words *daṭṭha daṭṭhabbaṃ* in the text to mean: "having seen, should be known" and explains the following words *diṭṭhaṃ na maññati* as a separate phrase meaning that the Tathāgata does not entertain any cravings, conceits or views, thinking: "I am seeing that which has been seen by the people." It applies the same mode of explanation throughout.
It is perhaps more plausible to explain *daṭṭha* or *diṭṭha* (vl. in Burmese MSS; see A II 25 fn. 3) as an ablative form of the past participle giving the sense: "as apart from sight;" and *daṭṭhabbaṃ diṭṭhaṃ* taken together would mean: "a visible thing." So also the other three corresponding terms: *sutā, mutā* and *viññātā*. The Buddha Jayanthi Tipiṭaka Series (No. 19, Sinhalese script) recognizes this reading but follows the commentary in rendering them as absolutives. The Chaṭṭha Saṅgīti Piṭaka edition (Burmese script), as well as the PTS edition, has the absoluteness form: *sutvā, mutvā* and *viññatvā*—which is probably a re-correction following the commentarial explanation.

This barb I beheld, well in advance,[20]
whereon mankind is hooked, impaled.
'I know, I see 'tis verily so'[21]*—no such clinging for the Tathāgatas."*

---

15. *Adiṭṭhaṃ na maññati*: according to the Comm. this means that the Tathāgata does not fancy (due to craving, etc.) he is seeing something which has not been seen by the people. But the expression seems to imply just the opposite. It brings out the idea behind the statement: "If I were to say: 'Monks, whatsoever in the world ... of ... gods and men—whatsoever is seen ... by the mind—all that I do not know,' it would be a falsehood in me."

16. *Daṭṭhabbaṃ na maññati*: here the full gerundival sense of the verb is evident. The Tathāgata does not consider any of those "sights" that people cherish, as "worth-while-seeing"—in the highest sense. He does not see anything substantial in them.

17. *Daṭṭhabbaṃ na maññati*: the Tathāgata does not entertain any conceit of being the agent behind seeing. When sights lose their object-status they do not reflect a "seer" on the subjective side.
These four modes of conceiving represent "the plane of voidness" (*suññata-bhūmi*).

18. *Tādi*: "such" or "such-like." An epithet of the emancipated one signifying his supreme detachment. This declaration indicates the plane of the "such one" (*tādi-bhūmi*).

CHAPTER III

Sign and Significance in Sense Perception

A clue to the difficulties experienced by the Buddha in coming to terms with the world may be found in your own unusual experience at the magic-show. To all intents and purposes you saw the magic performance. Yet, as your friend has proved to you, there are difficulties involved in any unreserved affirmation or denial. The position of a Tathāgata who has fully comprehended the magical illusion that is consciousness, is somewhat similar. He too has seen all the magical performances in the form of sense data enacted on the stage of consciousness. And yet he is aware of the limitations in any categorical affirmation or negation. Whereas the worldling is wont "to take his stand upon" the knowledge he has "grasped," the Tathāgata regards that

---

19. *Tesu … sayasaṃvutesu*: the Comm. says: "among those who are of (divers) views and who had grasped them having themselves recollected and cherished those view-points." The expression rather conveys the sense of self-opinionatedness due to philosophical in-breeding, and may be rendered by "among those who are restricted (*saṃvuta*) to their own views."

20. *Etañca sallaṃ paṭigacca disvā:* "Having seen this barb well in advance"—explained by the Commentary as the barb of views—which the Buddha saw in advance, at the foot of the Bodhi tree.

21. *Jānāmi passāmi tatheva etaṃ*: a phrase often cited in the Pali Canon as representing the stamp of dogmatism characteristic of speculative views. It is on a par with the dogmatic assertion: *idameva saccaṃ moghamaññaṃ* ("this alone is true, all else is false") which accompanies the formulation of the ten "unexplained points" (*avyākata-vatthūni*).

tendency as a "barb" in spite of (or because of) the fact that he has "fully understood."[22] In other words, he has seen the magic-show so well as to "miss the show" from the worldling's standpoint.

The question of "seeing what-is-shown," brings us to the relationship between sign and significance. Sense-perception at all levels relies largely on signs. This statement might even appear as a truism since the Pali word *saññā* (*Skt. saṃjnā*) denotes perception as well as "sign," "symbol," "mark" or "token." It is due to the processes of grasping and recognition implicit in sense-perception that the sign has come to play such an important part in it. Grasping—be it physical or mental—can at best be merely a symbolical affair. The actual point of contact is superficial and localized, but it somehow props up the conceit of grasping. Recognition, too, is possible only within arbitrarily circumscribed limits. The law of impermanence is persistently undermining it, but still a conceit of recognition is maintained by progressively

---

22. Note that the *raison d'etre* for the tetralemma type of formulation is this very detached attitude of the Buddha ("I know, I see 'tis verily so"—no such clinging for the Tathāgatas). If not for the reservation attached to the first alternative, he could have stopped at the second alternative, for a categorical affirmative requires only a categorical negation of the opposite standpoint. About the Kāḷakārāma Sutta one could say, as in the case of a magic-show, that "there-is-more-in-it-than-meets-the-eye." Normally, in a tetralemma the first alternative is negated. Here it is affirmed, but not categorically, for a reservation has been made. The added emphasis serves more or less a rhetorical purpose, showing that he not only knows what the world knows but has grown "wiser." The peculiarity in this formulation is a flashback to the *Mūlapariyāya Sutta* (MN 1) since the significance of the additional emphasis conveyed by the word *abbhaññāsiṃ* is distinctly revealed there by the use of the word *abhijānāti* while the reservation made regarding the first alternative finds its parallel there in the expression *na maññati*—an expression recurring in that exegetical type of disquisition which immediately follows the tetralemma in the *Kāḷakārāma Sutta*.

ignoring the fact of change. Thus both processes are kept up with the help of signs and symbols.

What do signs signify? "*Things* of course"—the less sophisticated would readily answer. As far as common sense goes, signs presumably stand for the "things" we perceive with their aid. And the "things" are those forms we see, the sounds we hear, the scents we smell, the flavours we taste, the objects we touch and the ideas we cognize. The more sophisticated would, however, prefer to be more precise. They would take up the position that behind those changing attributes that we perceive with our imperfect sense-apparatus, there lies an unchanging substance, an essence, a noumenon. Though analysis fails to reveal any such real essence, a "*Ding-an-sich*" under the ever-receding layers of qualities and attributes,[23] they would still maintain that, after all, there could not possibly be an attribute without a substance—a quality without a "thing" that it "qualifies."

According to the *Kāḷakārāma Sutta*, a Tathāgata does not conceive of a visible thing as apart from sight or an audible thing as apart from hearing or a thing to be sensed as apart from sensation or a cognizable thing as apart from cognition. Furthermore, as the Suttas often make it clear, all percepts as such are to be regarded as mere signs (*saññā, nimitta*).[24] Hence while the worldling says that he perceives "things" with the help of signs, the Tathāgata says that all we perceive are mere signs. Sights, sounds, smells, tastes, touches and ideas are, all of them, signs which consciousness pursues. But still the question may be asked: "What do these signs signify?" "Things, of course"—the Tathāgata would reply. "Things," however, are not those that the worldling has in mind when he seeks an answer to this question. Lust, hatred and delusion are the "things" which according to the teaching of the Tathāgata are signified by all sense-percepts.

---

23. "Perception is like a mirage"—See above, ch. I.
24. See S III 10, *Hāliddikāni Sutta*.

"Lust, friend, is a something, hatred is a something, delusion is a something." (*"Rāgo kho āvuso kiñcano, doso kiñcano, moho kiñcano"*—M 1298. *Mahāvedalla Sutta*), "Lust, friends is something significative, hatred is something significative, delusion is something significative" (*"Rāgo kho āvuso nimittakaraṇo, doso nimittakaraṇo, moho nimittakaraṇo"*—ibid.).

The pronouncement that all sense-percepts are signs and that the "things" they signify are lust, hatred and delusion might appear, at first sight, a not-too-happy blend of philosophy and ethics. But there are deeper implications involved. It is a fact often overlooked by the metaphysician that the reality attributed to sense-data is necessarily connected with their evocative power, that is, their ability to produce effects. The reality of a thing is usually registered in terms of its impact on the experiential side. This is the acid-test which an object is required to undergo to prove its existence in the court of reality. In the reference to materiality as "manifestative and offering resistance" (*sanidassana-sappaṭighaṃ rūpaṃ*—D III 217, *Saṅgīti Sutta*) the validity of this test seems to have been hinted at. Now, the "objects" of sense which we grasp and recognize as existing out there, derive their object-status from their impact or evocative power. Their ability to produce effects in the form of sense-reaction is generally taken to be the criterion of their reality. Sense-objects are therefore signs which have become significant in themselves owing to our ignorance that their significance depends on the psychological mainsprings of lust, hatred and delusion. This, in other words, is a result of reasoning from the wrong end (*ayoniso manasikāra*) which leads both the philosopher and the scientist alike into a topsy-turvydom of endless theorising.

Some reflection on your experiences at the magic-show might also give you an insight into the truth of the above pronouncement. To the audience steeped in the bliss of ignorance, the magic-show was full of significance, whatever you may say to the contrary. To them, all the articles and artifices employed by the magician—even the "hocus-pocus," the "abracadabra" and the waving of the magic-wand had a "reality" in the sense of their evocative power. The craned necks, the gazing eyes and gaping mouths bore inarticulate testimony to it. The "Ah!"s and "Oh!"s and whistles also expressed still inarticulately the "reality" of the magic-show. And last, but not least, that vivid commentary on the magic performance you had occasion to listen to soon after the show was the fully articulate expression of the "reality" of the bag of wily tricks presented by the shrewd magician. Behind all those gestures, exclamations and descriptions evoked by the "things" seen at the magic-show, you would not have failed to see the things that really were there—i.e., attachment, aversion and delusion.

CHAPTER IV

Dependent Arising—a via-media

The Buddha's insight into the backstage workings of the magic-show of consciousness has revealed to him the almost unbridgeable gulf that exists between his transcendental level of experience and the worldling's level of sense-experience. "Whatever, monks, that has been pondered over as truth by the world with its gods and Māras, by the progeny consisting of recluses and brahmins, gods and men, that has been well discerned as untruth by the noble ones, as it really is, with right wisdom"—this is one mode of reflection. "And whatever, monks, that has been pondered over as untruth by the world with its gods and Māras ... that has been well discerned as truth by the noble ones, as it really is, with right wisdom"—this is the second mode of reflection ... (Sn p. 147, *Dvayatānupassana Sutta*). "Monk, that which is of a deluding nature is indeed false and that is the truth, namely, Nibbāna, which is of a non-deluding nature. For, monk, this is the highest truth, namely, the non-delusive Nibbāna" (M III 245, *Dhātuvibhaṅga Sutta*). Despite such declarations by the Buddha of the wide disparity between the worldling's concept of truth and that of the noble ones, we find the *Kāḷakārāma Sutta* attributing to the Buddha himself a statement which seems to contradict those declarations. It says that the Tathāgata does not hold as true or false "whatever is seen, heard, sensed or clung to and is esteemed as truth by other folk." How can one resolve this paradox?

Once again, you may recollect your unusual experience at the magic-show. In that moment of compassion for the frenzied crowd applauding the magician, you had stumbled upon a wider concept of truth. It is the understanding of the principle of relativity behind the concept of truth. The realization that anyone placed in a similar situation would behave as that crowd had a mellowing effect on your sense of judgement. Given the same measure of ignorance as to the secrets of the magician, given the same psychological impulses of greed and hate, anyone would take up such a standpoint as that frenzied crowd and it is probably the same conviction that caused some embarrassment and hesitation in you in the course of that conversation with your friend. The same magic-show was seen in two different perspectives. While the audience saw what the magician performed, you from your point of vantage saw how he performed. Thus there were actually two levels of experience—one arising out of ignorance, the other out of knowledge. Each level carried with it its own conception of bliss, its own reactions and convictions. The former tended towards a tumultuous bliss of ignorance; the latter towards a bliss of appeasement born of understanding. In the Buddhist conception of the "knowledge-and-vision-of-things-as-they-are" (*yathā-bhūta-ñāṇa-dassana*) both levels of experience find a place. Its content is not any particular theory or a definite body of knowledge, but a norm which analyses and lays bare the very structure of experience. This is none other than the law of Dependent Arising (*paṭicca-samuppāda*), which in its direct order accounts for the former level of experience while recognizing at the same time the latter as well by its formulation in reverse order.

> "This being, that comes to be; with the arising of this that arises.
>
> This not being, that does not come to be; with the cessation of this, that ceases.
>
> "That is to say: From ignorance as condition (arise) formations; from formations as condition (arises) consciousness; from consciousness ... name-and-form, from name-and-form ... the six sense-spheres; from the six sense-spheres ... contact; from contact ... feeling; from feeling ... craving; from craving ... grasping; from

grasping ... becoming; from becoming ... birth; from birth as condition arise decay-and-death, sorrow, lamentation, pain, grief and despair. Such is the arising of this entire mass of suffering.

"From the complete fading away and cessation of that very ignorance, there comes to be the cessation of formations; from the cessation of formations, the cessation of consciousness; from the cessation of consciousness, the cessation of name-and-form; from the cessation of name-and-form, the cessation of the six sense-spheres; from the cessation of the six sense-spheres, the cessation of contact; from the cessation of contact, the cessation of feeling; from the cessation of feeling, the cessation of craving; from the cessation of craving, the cessation of grasping; from the cessation of grasping, the cessation of becoming; from the cessation of becoming, the cessation of birth. From the cessation of birth, decay-and-death, sorrow, lamentation, pain, grief and despair cease. Such is the ceasing of this entire mass of suffering" (M III, *Bahudhātuka Sutta*).

This law of Dependent Arising, which embraces the entire gamut of experience ranging from that of the worldling to the Arahant's, could be applied even to our problem of the magic-show. While the show was going on, if anyone had asked you and your friend: "Is there any magic?" he might have received two contradictory answers. Since, by then, the magic had lost its magic for you, you would have replied: "There is no magic," but your friend had the right to say: "There is." The two answers would be contradictory if understood in an absolute sense and asserted dogmatically without reference to the question of standpoint. The law of Dependent Arising resolves the above contradiction by avoiding the two extremes "is" and "is not" with its wise proviso: "It depends." Given the ignorance of the magician's tricks, formations (i.e., gestures, exclamations, imaginations) come to be; depending on these formations, the consciousness of the magic-show comes to be; dependent on this consciousness is "name-and-form" pertaining to the World of Magic (i.e., feeling, perception, intention, contact and attention constituting the "name" aspect and the four primaries of solidity, liquidity, heat and air together with the derivative concept of form making up the "form" aspect of the World of Magic); depending on this "name-and-form" which comprehends the entire stock-in-trade of the magician, the six sense-spheres of the deluded audience are kept all agog with curiosity; depending on these sense-spheres there arise appropriate impressions of the marvellous World of Magic; conditioned by such impressions feelings of exhilaration arise; from these feelings there develops a craving for the perpetuation of that very exhilaration; in response to that craving, there comes to be a grasping after the magic-performances; from that grasping there results a chimerical existence in a "world-of magic" and the audience, thus spell-bound, finds itself "born," as it were, into a "wonderland." This "birth," however, is short-lived. The marvellous magic-show too, "like all good things," comes to an end, and that is its decay-and-death.

The above illustration would have made it clear that the existence of the magic can neither be affirmed nor denied absolutely. And what is true of the magic is true of all phenomena comprising the magic-show of consciousness. The fact that existence is a relative concept is often overlooked by the worldling. Says the Buddha: "This world, Kaccāyana, usually bases (its views) on two things: on existence and non-existence. Now, he who with right insight sees the arising of the world as it really is does not hold with the non-existence of the world. And he who with right insight sees the passing away of the world as it really is does not hold with the existence of the world. The world, for the most part, is given to approaching, grasping, entering into and getting entangled (as regards views). Whoever does not approach, grasp and take his stand upon that proclivity towards approaching and grasping, that mental standpoint—namely, the thought: 'This is my soul'—he knows that what arises is just suffering and what ceases is just suffering. Thus he is not in doubt, is not perplexed and herein he has knowledge that is not dependent on another. Thus far, Kaccāyana, he has right view. 'Everything exists,' this is one extreme. 'Nothing exists,' this is the other extreme. Not approaching either of those extremes, the Tathāgata teaches the Dhamma by the middle way: From ignorance as condition formations come to be; from formations as condition consciousness comes to be ... Such is the arising of this entire mass of suffering. From the complete fading away and cessation of that very ignorance, there comes to be the cessation of formations; from the cessation of formations, the cessation of consciousness ... Such is the cessation of this entire mass of suffering."—S II 17, *Kaccāyanagotta Sutta*.

In the context of the law of Dependent Arising, therefore, the unusual statement of the *Kāḷakārāma Sutta* appears to be quite legitimate. To take up—as the worldling does—a standpoint with regard to "whatever is seen, heard, sensed, cognized, attained, sought after and pondered over by the mind" is alien to the spirit behind this comprehensive psychological principle. The Buddha realized that all worldly theories and viewpoints are but "individual truths" in which people are severally entrenched (*paccekasaccesu puthū niviṭṭhā*—Sn 824). Dogmatic theories asserted as absolute truths were regarded by him as a "barb" on which mankind is hooked and impaled." The worldly concepts of truth and falsehood have a questionable background. They are but the outcome of sense-perception and are beaten out on the anvil of logic in the process of moulding this or that theory. "There exist no diverse truths which in the world are eternal, apart from perception. Having formulated theories in accordance with logic, they have arrived at the twofold categories called "the true" and "the false."" (Sn 886). The medley of speculative theories were but partial truths in so far as they originated from individual experience coloured by a good deal of prejudice. The *Aṭṭhakavagga* of the Suttanipāta, in particular, analyses the psychology behind the worldling's value judgements as to truth and falsehood. Led by prejudice,[25] he develops a concept of truth out of his viewpoint and tests its validity in debate, where the triple-conceit, "equal," "superior" and "inferior," decides the issue.[26] The Buddha points out that if victory in debate is the criterion, truth becomes a mere matter of opinion. "Not indeed do I say that this is valid whereby they mutually called each other fools. They consider their own dogmatic view as the truth; hence do they call the other a fool" (Sn 882).

The self-opinionatedness on which debates thrive is sometimes the result of an alleged spiritual experience. And then it would come out in a dogmatic tone: "I know, I see, it is verily so" (*jānāmi passāmi tatheva etaṃ*—Sn 908.[26] If the opponent too is prompted by such an experience which has led him to a different conclusion, we get an irreconcilable conflict, a classic instance of which is found in the following words of two brahmin sophists:

"Purāṇa Kassapa, O sire Gotama, claims to be omniscient and all-seeing; he claims to have perfect knowledge and vision, saying: 'While walking, standing, sleeping and lying awake, knowledge and vision are ever-present to me.' And he has declared: 'I abide knowing and seeing an infinite world with an infinite knowledge.' But Gotama, this Nigaṇṭha Nāthaputta too, claims to be omniscient and all-seeing; he too claims to have perfect knowledge and vision saying: 'While walking, standing, sleeping and lying awake, knowledge and vision are ever present to me.' And he has declared: 'I abide knowing and seeing a finite world with a finite knowledge.' Out of these

---

25. *Chandanunito ruciyā niviṭṭho*—Sn 781. "Led by desire and possessed by inclinations."
26. See *Gūhaṭṭhaka, Duṭṭhaṭṭhaka, Suddhaṭṭhaka, Paramaṭṭhaka, Pasura, Māgandiya, Kalahavivāda, Cūḷaviyūha* and *Mahāviyūha Suttas* of the *Aṭṭhaka Vagga*.

two professors of knowledge, sire Gotama, who contradict each other, which one has spoken the truth and which one the falsehood?"—A IV 428 f.

The Buddha, however, refuses to act as arbiter in this conflict of viewpoints. Instead, he says: "Enough O brahmins, let that be.[27] Let be your question: "Out of these two professors of knowledge who contradict each other, which one has spoken the truth and which one the falsehood?" Brahmins, I will preach to you the Dhamma. Listen attentively ... And he did preach it, pointing out, in the course of it, that in the terminology of the noble ones, "the world" is defined as the five strands of sense-pleasures and that the "end of the world" is Arahantship itself.

One might wonder why the Buddha set aside such a clear-cut question. For one thing, "the world," according to the Buddha, had to be redefined, so as to bring out its phenomenal nature. But there is probably another reason. Both worthies involved in this contest for supremacy claimed omniscience, but whereas the former saw "an infinite world with an infinite knowledge" the latter saw "a finite world with a finite knowledge."[28] Now, the former could, within the bounds of logic, point out a flaw in the latter's position: "You

---

27. The expression *tiṭṭhatetaṃ* indicates that the question belongs to the type called *ṭhapanīya-pañhā* (i.e., "questions that should be set aside")—one of the four types into which all questions are classified by the Buddha, the other three being: *ekaṃsa-vyākaraṇīya* ("questions which admit of a categorical reply") *paṭipuccha-vyākaraṇīya* ("those that need counter-questioning"), and *vibhajja-vyākaraṇīya* ("those requiring an analytical statement"). A set of ten questions thus set aside by him are technically called *avyākata-vatthūni* ("unexplained points") and the two viewpoints appear there too, in the following form: "Is the world finite? Is the world infinite?"

28. The text shows a bewildering number of variant readings, "mutually contradicting each other." Perhaps the interpretation attempted here will provide a clue to the correct reading as to the two viewpoints in question.

are seeing a finite world because your knowledge *is limited* (i.e., finite)." The latter too can rejoin, with equal justification: "But you are seeing an infinite world because your knowledge *lacks finality* (i.e., infinite)." In other words, while the former can regard the latter's knowledge as imperfect on the ground that he cannot see beyond what he claims to be "the end-of-the-world," the latter can hold the former's knowledge to be imperfect, saying that "the end-of-the-world" is beyond its range.

This is the kind of circularity in argument often found in speculative views put forward by worldly philosophers.[29] Those who held on to them dogmatically are compared to the blind men who fell out and came to blows when their individual views on what an elephant looks like clashed with each other (Ud 66 ff.).

There is, however, one truth knowing which people would not dispute,[30] and that is the very synoptic understanding of the arising, the passing-away, the satisfaction, the misery and the "stepping-out" in regard to that sense-experience on which all speculative theories are founded. "And that, monks, the Tathāgata understands thus: 'These viewpoints thus taken up, thus laid hold of will have such and such consequences, will lead to such and such future states of existence.' That the Tathāgata understands; and he understands even beyond that. But that understanding he does not grasp; and not grasping, he has, within himself, known the appeasement (*nibbuti*). Having known, as they really are, the arising, the passing-away, the satisfaction, the misery and the "stepping-out" in regard to feelings, monks, released without grasping is the Tathāgata" (D I 21 ff., *Brahmajāla Sutta*).

29. See also M II 32 ff., *Cūḷasakuludāyi Sutta*.
30. *Ekaṃ hi saccaṃ na dutiyaṃ atthi, yasmiṃ pajā no vivade pajānaṃ*—Sn 884.
"For the truth is one and there is no second, having an insight into which the people would not enter into dispute."

CHAPTER V

The Vortical Interplay— Consciousness versus Name-and-form

The most outstanding contribution made by the law of Dependent Arising to the ethical, psychological and philosophical enquiries of all times, is the revelation that there is a vortex hidden beneath the flux of all mental life. Perpetually supporting each other and revitalising each other as they go doting round and round, "consciousness" and "name-and-form" make up the saṃsāric vortex which is the rallying point of all existence.

I. "Just as if, friend, two bundles of reeds were to stand one supporting the other, even so consciousness is dependent on name-and-form and name-and-form is dependent on consciousness; and the six sense-spheres on name-and-form, contact on the six sense-spheres, feeling on contact, craving on feeling, grasping on craving, becoming on grasping, birth on becoming and decay-and-death, sorrow, lamentation, pain, grief and despair are dependent on birth. Thus is the arising of this entire mass of suffering. But, friend, if one of those two bundles of reeds is drawn out, the other one would fall down, and if the latter is drawn out the former one will fall down. Even so, friend, with the cessation of name-and-form, consciousness ceases; with the cessation of consciousness, name-and-form ceases; with the cessation of name-and-form, the six sense-spheres cease ... Thus comes to be the cessation of this entire mass of suffering" (S II 114, *Naḷakalāpī Sutta*).

II. "This consciousness turns back from name-and-form, it does not go beyond. In so far can one be born or grow old or die or pass away or reappear, in so far as this is, to wit: Consciousness is dependent on name-and-form, name-and-form on consciousness, the six sense-spheres on name-and-form ... Thus comes to be the arising of this entire mass of suffering"[31] (D II 32, *Mahāpadāna Sutta*).

III. "In so far only, Ānanda, can one be born or grow old, or die or pass away or reappear, in so far only is there any pathway for verbal expression, in so far only is there any

---

31. The traditional "three-life" interpretation of the formula of *paṭicca samuppāda* which refers the first two links to a past existence, perceives a difficulty here: "When there is name-and-form, there is consciousness:" here it should also have been mentioned that consciousness is there when formations are there and that formations are there when ignorance is there. But both of them have not been taken in here. Hence ignorance and formations represent the past existence. This insight does not connect itself with them, for the Great Being is concerned with the present. Is it not a fact that so long as ignorance and formations remain unrecognized one cannot become a Buddha? True, one cannot. But at this point the exposition of Dependent Arising has to be given in detail to show that they (i.e., the aforesaid two links) were seen by him in the form of (the three links) "becoming," "grasping" and "craving." That exposition, however, has already been given in the *Visuddhimagga*" (D-a).

This difficulty would not arise when we identify consciousness and name-and-form as the vortex of all saṃsāric existence—past, present and future. Since it is "in so far only" that there is the range of wisdom (*ettāvatā paññāvacaram*), there is no possibility of going beyond. It is the very ignorance of this vortex that constitutes the first link in the formula, and the deluded vortical interplay arising out of it, is the second link (i.e., formations). With the proper understanding of this situation the meaningless interplay is made to cease. Thus there is nothing actually missing in the *Mahāpadāna Sutta*.

The law of Dependent Arising is a Noble Norm (*ariyo nayo*) which in all its twelve-linked completeness is well-seen and well-penetrated through wisdom (*paññāya sudiṭṭho hoti suppaṭividdho*) even by a Stream-winner (*sotāpanna*), who may not possess the knowledge of past lives. (See A V 184).

pathway for terminology, in so far only is there any pathway for designations, in so far only is the range of wisdom, in so far only is the round (of saṃsāric life) kept going for there to be any designation of the conditions of this existence; that is to say, name-and-form together with consciousness" (D II 63f. *Mahā Nidāna Sutta*).

In this interplay between the two counterparts, consciousness seems to represent actuality while name-and-form[32] stands for potentiality. "Name-and-form" when it "grows up" (see D II 63) deriving vitality from consciousness, gives rise to the infra-structure of the six sense-bases or spheres, which undergo bifurcation as "internal" (*ajjhattika*) and "external" (*bāhira*) due to the discriminative function of consciousness. The ensuing processes of contact, feeling, craving, grasping and becoming portray the springing up into life of those potentialities indicated by name-and-form. With "becoming" (*bhava*) the vicious circle is complete and "birth" is born carrying with it the unpleasant prospects of decay-and-death, sorrow, lamentation, pain, grief and despair. The two links, ignorance and formations, though they are not mentioned in the above three passages, are nevertheless implicit, for the murk of ignorance provides the background for this interplay while formations directly manifest themselves as the prelude to, and the motive force behind, the narcissistic interplay.

By way of illustration, we may, for a moment, turn to a game of cricket. Here consciousness recognizes the presence of two sides as a precondition for the game, while "name-and-form" represents the rules, the procedure and the paraphernalia of the game.[33] The six sense-spheres which consciousness bifurcates into "internal" and "external" are the actual teams selected for the game. With contact, feeling,

32. "Feeling, perception, intention, contact, attention—these, O friends, are called 'name.' The four great elements and form dependent on them, these, O friends, are called 'form.'"—M I 53, *Sammādiṭṭhi Sutta*.

craving, grasping and becoming, the cricket-match is in full swing. And "birth-decay-and-death" etc. more or less represent the inexorable vicissitudes of the game. That all pathways for verbal expression, terminology and designation converge on the vortex of consciousness and name-and-form is also amply illustrated by this analogy, since the significance of the game depends on one's being conscious of it as a cricket-match, with all its implications regarding the personnel, paraphernalia and rules involved.

In the wider context of our saṃsāric existence, the vortical interplay between consciousness and name-and-form manifests itself as a kind of double-bind (*jāta*)—"a tangle within" and "a tangle without."[34] Consciousness as the subject always finds itself confronted with "name-and-form" as the object, depending on which it develops the concepts of resistance (*paṭigha*) and form (*rūpasaññā*). An interplay follows which is as much comic as it is tragic in that it involves a *petitio principii*—an assertion of existence that is equivalent to "begging the question."

Since the criterion of reality of a thing is, as mentioned above (see Ch. III), the very impact it has on one's experiential side, the worldling's proneness to cling to "name-and-form" as real, may be explained with reference to "contact" (*phassa*), which is dependent on it. According to the Buddha, contact is itself a hybrid manifesting traits proper to both groups designated as "name" and "form." The following disquisition

---

33. Perhaps it will not be inapt to identify the five constituents of "name"—i.e., I. contact, II. feeling, III. perception, IV. intention and V. attention—with the following aspects of the game, respectively: I. competition, II. elation, depression or boredom in the course of the game, III. the scoreboard, IV. prospect of winning, V. watching the game. "Form," in this connection, would consist of the personnel and paraphernalia involved in the game.

34. *Anto jaṭā bahi jaṭā, jaṭāya jaṭitā pajā*—S I 13, *Jaṭā Sutta*. "A tangle within, a tangle without. This world is entangled in a tangle."

on this particular aspect of the problem is likely to be of immense value to the modern psychologist and philosopher.

"'From name-and-form as condition, contact comes to be,[35]' thus it has been said above. And that, Ānanda, should be understood in this manner, too, as to how, from name-and-form as condition, contact arises. If, Ānanda, all those modes, characteristics, signs and exponents by which the name-group (*nāma-kāya*) is designated were absent, would there be manifest any verbal impression (*adhivacana-samphassa*) in the form group (*rūpa-kāya*)?"

"There would not, Lord."

"If, Ānanda, all those modes, characteristics, signs and exponents by which the form-group is designated were absent, would there be manifest any resistance-impression (*paṭigha-samphassa*) in the name-group?"

"There would not, Lord."

"And if, Ānanda, all those modes, characteristics, signs and exponents by which there is a designation of both name-group and form-group were absent, would there be manifest either any verbal-impression or any resistance-impression?"

"There would not, Lord."

"And if, Ānanda, all those modes, characteristics, signs and exponents by which there comes to be a designation of name-and-form were absent, would there be manifest any contact?"

"There would not, Lord."

"Wherefore, Ānanda, this itself is the cause, this is the origin, this is the condition, for contact, that is to say, name-and-form" (D II 62, *Mahā Nidāna Sutta*).

The relevance of signs to this subject of contact is recognized throughout this disquisition. Both the name-group and the form-group derive their respective designations with the help of "modes, characteristics, signs

---

35. The six sense-spheres are omitted here but their role is sufficiently implicit in this comprehensive treatment of contact. Note that the six sense-spheres see often called: *chaphassāyatanāni*.

and exponents." But the most extraordinary fact about them is that their significance depends on each other—a curious reciprocity. A verbal-impression in regard to the form-group is at all possible because there are those modes, characteristics, etc. proper to the name-group. The concept of form is established only when the constituents of the name-group (i.e., contact, feeling, perception, intention, attention) have sufficiently "experimented" with it. Even the so-called four great elements or primaries are themselves subject to this test of validity without which they simply could not stand. Thus earth, water, fire and air actually represent the experiences of solidity, liquidity, heat and motion, in which the name-group plays its part. As "elements" they are mere abstractions, but they come within the purview of contact as "form" or "matter" (*rūpa*) in the guise of verbal-impression[36] which distinguishes between them according to the degree of predominance of their respective qualities. The name-group, for its part, owes its validity to the modes, characteristics, etc., proper to the form-group. The notion of resistance or impact goes hand in hand with the concept of form or matter, since the "actual" impact (i.e., impact par excellence) as something that "matters," is generally associated with "matter." ("Seeing is believing, but touch is the real thing!"). Hence contact, feeling, perception, intention and attention find "actual" objects in the world of matter. In other words, impact or sense-reaction is primarily associated with the signs proper to the form-group (*paṭigha-samphassa*) and only secondarily and metaphorically, with those of the name-group (*adhivacana-samphassa*). This complex character of name-and-form in relation to contact indicates that Buddhism does not recognize a dichotomy between mind and matter. Instead, it reveals that mentality and materiality are inextricably interwoven into "a tangle-within" and a "tangle-without."

---

36. "The four great elements, monk, are the cause, the four great elements are the condition for the designation of the aggregate of form."—M III 17, *Mahāpuṇṇama Sutta*.

Name-and-form is seen to play a dual role. In organic combination with consciousness, it is already found in the individual as implied by the expression *saviññāṇaka-kāya* ("the conscious-body"). This is the tangle within. As a thing to be measured with this "conscious body," name-and-form is also projected outside into signs (*nimitta*) in need of interpretation or evaluation. The "internal" sense-bases and the "external" sense-bases both partake of name-and-form. The "measuring-unit" and the thing measured thus presuppose each other, as one may infer from the following Sutta passages:

I. "Name," friends, is one end, "form" is the other end; consciousness is in the middle; and craving is the seamstress, for it is craving that stitches it into the arising of this and that (form of) existence ..."—A III 400.

II. "The six internal sense-spheres are one end, the six external sense-spheres are the other end, consciousness is in the middle; and craving is the seamstress ... (ibid.).

III. "For the fool, monks, cloaked by ignorance and tied to craving, this body is wrought in this way: There is this body (*ayañceva kāyo*) and name-and-form without (*bahiddhā ca nāmarūpaṃ*)—thus this pair. Because of the pair there is contact and just six spheres of sense"—S II 23f.

IV. "How, Lord, does one know, how does one see, so that in regard to both this conscious body (*imasmiñca saviññāṇake kāye*) and also all external signs (*bahiddhā ca sabbanimittesu*), the mind has gone away from notions of "I" and "mine" and from vain conceits, transcending all distinctions (*vidha-samatikkantaṃ*), is at peace and well released?"—S II 253.

In the context of these two "tangles," any rigid dichotomy between "mind" and "matter" such as is envisaged by the worldly philosophers, would appear to be an oversimplification of facts. Any attempt at solving the problem by taking up an exclusive idealistic or a realistic attitude is bound to fail. The only solution, in the opinion of the Buddha, lay in cutting off completely this "Gordian knot":

> *Wherein are cut off name and form*
> *Sense-reaction and precepts of form*
> *Leaving no residue at all*
> *Therein is cut off the tangle withal.*[37]

The trends that set in with the vortical interplay between consciousness and name-and-form continue through the subsequent links of the formula of Dependent Arising. The six sense-spheres bifurcate themselves precipitating, a dichotomy of an "internal" and an "external" with its concomitant notions of a "here" and a "there." Contact, in a specific sense, is a sequel to this very dichotomy. It implies a principle of discrimination between two things and consciousness fulfils this condition. "Dependent on the eye and forms, friends, there arises eye-consciousness, a coming together of the three is contact ... (M I 111, *Madhupiṇḍika Sutta*). The canonical simile of the friction between two sticks[38] illustrates this aspect of contact. With feeling, the split in experience becomes sufficiently palpable as to call forth the notion: "I am." "Where, friend, there is no feeling at all, would there be any such notion as: 'I am'?" "There would not, Lord" (D II 67, *Mahānidāna Sutta*). The

---

37. *Yattha nāmañca rūpañca—asesaṃ uparujjhati / paṭighaṃ rūpasaññā ca—ettha sa chijjate jaṭā*—S I 13, *Jaṭā Sutta*.

38. "Just as, monks, from the coming together of two sticks by way of friction, there arises heat and fire is produced, and by the separation, the laying aside, of these two sticks themselves, whatever heat was born thereof that ceases, subsides. Even so, monks, these three feelings (see below) are born of contact, rooted in contact, arisen out of contact, dependent on contact. Depending on a specific contact, specific feelings arise and with the cessation of a specific contact specific feelings cease."—S IV 215, *Phassamūlaka Sutta*.

Compare this simile with what was said above regarding the "actual impact."

discriminative function of consciousness is seen here in the form of distinguishing three feeling-tones and hence sometimes one finds consciousness itself being defined in terms of knowing discriminatively (*vijānāti*) the three grades of feeling—"pleasant" (*sukha*), "unpleasant" (*dukkha*) and "neither-unpleasant-nor-pleasant" (*adukkhamasukha*).[39] Out of this discrimination there arises craving (or "thirst") for the pleasant and consequently, a reaching-out—a "grasping" for the same. In the process of "grasping" there is involved a kind of "projection" of desires (cf. *nati*—"inclination, bent") whereby the split in experience widens into a definite gap between a subject and an object. "Becoming" or "existence" is the make-believe attempt to bridge this gap which, however, forever remains unbridged, for the material on which it relies is perpetually crumpling up underneath. Yet it somehow props up the conceit of an ego—the conceit "I am" (*asmimāna*). From the point of view of the ego, the things clung to (*upādāna*) appear as assets (*upadhi*) and one takes pride in the very things one depends on. Thus liabilities are looked upon as positive assets and an abject slavery becomes a petty mastery. The topsy-turvydom is complete and the double-bind becomes a fait accompli. The ego now finds itself "born" into a world of likes and dislikes, subject to decay-and-death, sorrow, lamentation, pain, grief and despair.

---

39. See M I 292, *Mahāvedalla Sutta*.

Chapter VI

"Self"—The Point-of-View

The birth of the "ego" or "self" as an "individual"[40] out of the vortical interplay is at the same time the birth of a "point-of-view." Personality-view (*sakkāyadiṭṭhi*—lit. the "existing-body" view) in its twenty modes portrays the desperate attempt of the illusory self to build for itself a foundation by grasping the five aggregates, though these are all the time disintegrating.

"Supposing, monks, there were a river, a mountain-torrent, a swift-flowing stream that goes a long way. On both its banks there might be growing kusa-grass that overhangs, babbaja-grass that overhangs, bīrana-grass that overhangs, trees that overhang. A man being swept away by that stream might clutch at the kusa-grass, but it might break away and owing to that he would come to grief. He might clutch at the babbaja-grass ... He might clutch at the bīrana-grass ... He might clutch at the trees but they too might break away and owing to that he would come to grief.

"Even so, monks, the uninstructed ordinary man who takes no account of the Noble Ones, is unskilled in the Dhamma of the Noble Ones, untrained in the Dhamma of the Noble Ones, taking no account of the good men, unskilled in the Dhamma of the good men, untrained in the Dhamma of

---

40. "And what, monks, is birth? That which of this and that being, in this and that species, is birth, arising, descent (i.e., conception), coming into existence, appearance of aggregates, acquiring of sense-spheres. This is called birth."—S II 3. "Birth," in its broadest sense, is applicable even to "gold and silver" (*jātarūparajataṃ*) according to the *Ariyapariyesana Sutta* (M I 162), for all "assets" are subject to birth (*Jātidhammā h'ete bhikkhave upadhayo*—ibid.).

the good men, looks upon form as self, or self as having form, or form as being in self, or self as being in form. But his form disintegrates and owing to that he would come to grief. And so with feeling, perception, formations and consciousness ..."—S III 137, *Nadi Sutta* ("The River").

It is the tragedy of the double-bind that despite their transient nature the five groups sustain the individual's conceit "I am," even as a mirror reflects the image of one who gazes at it.

"Owing to dependence, friend Ānanda, comes the conceit 'I am,' not without dependence. Depending on what comes the conceit 'I am?' Depending on form there comes the conceit 'I am,' not otherwise. Depending on feeling ... perception ... formations ... Depending on consciousness there comes the conceit 'I am,' not otherwise. Just as, friend Ānanda, a young woman or man fond of self-adornment, in gazing at the image of her or his face in a clean spotless mirror or in a bowl of clear water, does so depending on something and not without depending, even so, friend Ānanda, depending on form comes the conceit 'I am,' not otherwise. Depending on feeling ... perception ... formations ... Depending on consciousness comes the conceit "I am," not otherwise."—S III 105, *Ānanda Sutta*.

If, in the ignorant worldling's reflection, "selfhood" appears as something self-evident, it is due to this predicament in which he finds himself. The self-image follows him like a shadow that can neither be outstripped nor escaped. Hence one can sympathize with the "self"—created problems of both the Eternalist and the Nihilist. The Eternalist's discomfiture in the face of impermanence is easily understood but perhaps not so easily the Nihilist's. He is dismayed to find the "self" which he vehemently denied dogging him close behind, when he turns back to introspect. Thus whether one takes up the viewpoint "I have a soul" or the opposite viewpoint, "I do not have a soul" he is bound either way.[41]

"... Monks, a Tathāgata understands that thus: 'There are recluses and brahmins who make known an existing being's annihilation, obliteration and non-being. Because of fear of the existing body (*sakkāya*), because of disgust with the existing body, they keep running round, keep circling round, that same existing-body. Just as a dog tethered by a leash and anchored to a stout pole or post keeps running round, keeps circling round, that same pole or post, so too these worldly recluses and brahmins, because of fear of the existing body, because of disgust with the existing-body, keep running round, keep circling round, that same existing-body ..."[42]—M II 232f., *Pañcattaya Sutta*.

Since the obsession of self persists whether one runs towards the shadow or away from it, the solution advanced

---

41. In the *Sabbāsava Sutta* (M I 8) the Buddha includes these two among the six views which are said to arise in one who wrongly reflects in the following manner: "Was I in the past? Was I not in the past? What was I in the past? How was I in the past? Having been what, what was I in the past? Shall I be in the future? Shall I not be in the future? What shall I be in the future? How shall I be in the future? Having been what, what shall I be in the future?" Or else, he is doubtful in himself about the present, thus: "Am I? Am I not? What am I? How am I? Whence has this being come? Whither will it be bound?"

This kind of reflection leads one into a jungle of views because one has taken for granted the "I." The proper reflection is in terms of the Four Noble Truths, since all that exists and ceases is suffering.

The two questions of Vacchagotta (S IV 400f.): "Is there a soul?" or "Is there no soul?" carried the same presumptions born of wrong reflection. Hence the Buddha's silence. As the Buddha, for his part, had no conception of a soul which is but a figment of the worldling's imagination, he used to negate it only where it was asserted with specific reference to one or the other of the aggregates. Thus, for instance, before he ventured to answer Poṭṭhapāda's question: "Is perception a man's soul or is perception one thing and soul another?" he counter-questioned him: "What do you mean by a soul?"—D I 185f., *Poṭṭhapāda Sutta*.

by the Buddha was the comprehension of the very conditioned nature of the five aggregates of grasping, thereby recognizing the shadow for what it is.

"He who sees Dependent Arising sees the Dhamma, and he who sees the Dhamma sees Dependent Arising. These are but dependently arisen, namely, the five aggregates of grasping. That desire, attachment, involvement and entanglement in regard to these five aggregates of grasping, is the arising of suffering and that disciplining, that giving up, of desire-and-lust in these five aggregates of grasping, is the cessation of suffering."—M I 191, *Mahāhatthipadopama Sutta.*

By seeing things as they are in the light of wisdom, one comes to understand that the shadow is cast by a narrow point-of-view in the murk of ignorance. This vision or insight is the result of the arising of the dustless, stainless "Eye of Truth" (*virajaṃ vītamalaṃ dhammacakkhuṃ*)—also called the "Eye-of-Wisdom" (*paññācakkhu*)—which reveals to the Stream-Winner, the Noble Norm summed up in the words "Whatever is of a nature to arise, all that is of a nature to cease" (*"kiñci samudayadhammaṃ sabbaṃ tam nirodhadhammaṃ"*—M I 380, *Upāli Sutta*). The disillusionment brought about by this extraordinary vision is so pervasive and transforming that the Buddha compares it to the case of a congenitally blind man who, as soon as he gains eyesight, becomes disillusioned about a greasy grimy cloth with which he had been deceived. And even as that man would regard with disfavour the trickster who gave him the cloth saying that it is a beautiful piece of pure white cloth, the Noble Disciple too, on gaining the "Eye of Truth," undergoes a change of attitude towards his own mind: "… Even so, Māgandiya, if I were to teach you the Dhamma, pointing out to you that state of health—that Nibbāna—and if you, on your part, were to understand that state of health and see that Nibbāna, simultaneous with that arising of the eye in you,

42. The translation (with minor alterations) is from Venerable Ñāṇamoli's unpublished Majjhima Nikāya translation.

whatever desire-and-lust you had in the five aggregates of grasping will be abandoned. And furthermore, it would occur to you: "For a long time, indeed, have I been cheated, deceived and enticed by this mind; for, in grasping, it was merely form that I had been grasping, it was merely feeling that I had been grasping, it was merely perception that I had been grasping, it was merely formations that I had been grasping, it was merely consciousness that I had been grasping. And from my grasping there arises becoming; conditioned by becoming, birth; and conditioned by birth there arise decay-and-death, sorrow, lamentation, pain, grief, despair. It is thus that there comes to be the arising of this entire mass of suffering."—M I 511f., *Māgandiya Sutta*.

Your own disenchantment on seeing through the wily tricks of the magician might give an indication of the nature of the transformation in outlook that results from the arising of the Eye of Truth. The Noble Disciple too begins to discover the magician's "surprises" well in advance so as to be able to anticipate the "surprises." The magic loses its magic for him, now that he sees plainly where exactly the secret of the magic lies—that is, in his own psychological mainsprings of lust, hatred and delusion. He realizes that, apart from them, there is no reality in the articles and artifices involved in the magic-show of consciousness, and is now in a position to appreciate the Buddha's statement in the *Kāḷakārāma Sutta*: "Thus, monks, a Tathāgata does not conceive of a visible thing as apart from sight; he does not conceive of an unseen; he does not conceive of a "thing-worth-seeing"; he does not conceive about a seer ..."

The penetration into the conditioned nature of consciousness is tantamount to a storming of the citadel of the illusory self. With it, the "personality-view" (*sakkāyadiṭṭhi*) is abandoned and the "assets" (*upadhi*) on which the "self" depended—i.e., the five aggregates of grasping—begin to get liquidated. Consciousness ceases to appear as a substantial core of living experience. Instead, one now sees it with radical reflection (*yoniso manasikāra*) as a dependently arisen phenomenon which is always specific, even as fire is. "Just as, monks, dependent on whatever condition a fire burns, it comes to be reckoned in terms of that condition (that is to say), a fire that burns dependent on logs is reckoned as a 'log-fire'; a fire that burns dependent on faggots is reckoned as a 'faggot-fire'; a fire that burns dependent on grass is reckoned as a 'grass-fire'; a fire that burns dependent on cow-dung is reckoned as a 'cow-dung fire'; a fire that burns dependent on chaff is reckoned as a 'chaff fire'; a fire that burns dependent on rubbish is reckoned as a 'rubbish-fire'—even so, monks, consciousness is reckoned by the condition dependent on which it arises. A consciousness arising dependent on eye and forms is reckoned as 'an eye-consciousness'; a consciousness arising dependent on ear and sounds is reckoned as 'an ear-consciousness'; a consciousness arising dependent on nose and smells is reckoned as 'a nose-consciousness'; a consciousness arising dependent on tongue and flavours is reckoned as 'a tongue-consciousness'; a consciousness arising dependent on body and tangibles is reckoned as 'a body-consciousness'; a consciousness arising dependent on mind and ideas is reckoned as 'a mind-consciousness.'"—M I 259f., *Mahātaṇhāsaṅkhaya Sutta*.

The five aggregates which, from the point of view of self, one earlier took for granted as "the given," now appear as "dependently-arisen," "made-up" and "composite." Their process of accumulation (*upacaya*) is also seen to be something like a trickling through the sieve of consciousness. But even the sieve of consciousness performs its function only when the proper conditions are there. "If the eye in oneself, friends, were intact, but no external forms entered the range of vision and there were no appropriate[43] bringing into focus (*samannāhāro*), then there would be no manifestation of the appropriate class of consciousness. If the eye in oneself were intact and external forms also entered the range of vision but

43. I.e., *tajjo*: conveying the sense of specificity. See S IV 215 at p. 34, n. 38.

there were no appropriate focussing, there would be no manifestation of the appropriate class of consciousness. But it is when the eye in oneself is intact, external forms also enter the range of vision and the appropriate focussing too is there, that there is a manifestation of the appropriate class of consciousness. And any form in one who is in such a state is included in the form-aggregate of grasping; any feeling in him is included in the feeling-aggregate of grasping; any perception in him is included in the perception-aggregate of grasping; any formation in him is included in the formations-aggregate of grasping and any consciousness in him is included in the consciousness-aggregate of grasping. And he understands: 'This, it seems, is how there comes to be inclusion, gathering and amassing into these five aggregates of grasping.'"—M I 190, *Mahāhatthipadopama Sutta*.

CHAPTER VII

The Transcendental Path

A flash of insight might give one a glimpse of the subtle back-stage manoeuvres behind the illusory magic-show of consciousness, but in every case it might not be powerful enough to destroy all cankers or influxes (*āsava*) which seek to influence every moment of one's living experience.[44] The influxes, which are generally reckoned to be threefold[45]—i.e., those of sensuality (*kāmāsavā*), becoming (*bhavāsavā*) and ignorance (*avijjāsavā*) are the cankers born of our cumulative experience in saṃsāra. They include all corrupting tendencies, inclinations and obsessions that constitute the ruts and grooves of our mental terrain. Perhaps a deeper analysis of their influence is to be seen in the seven latencies (*anusaya*)—those of attachment, aversion, views, doubts, conceits, attachment-to-becoming and ignorance. If latencies are to be compared to subterranean currents at subconscious level, influxes might be described as streams manifest at the conscious level. In the ethical terminology of early Buddhism

---

44. "It is as if, friend, there were in the desert path a well, and neither rope nor drawer of water. And a man should come by oppressed with heat, foredone with heat, weary, parched, thirsty. He should look down into the well. Verily, in him would be the knowledge: "Water!"—Yet he would not be in a position to touch it physically.

"Even so, friend, I have well seen by right insight as it really is that the ceasing of becoming is Nibbāna, and yet I am not an Arahant in whom influxes are extinct"—S II 118, *Kosambi Sutta*.

45. Sometimes *diṭṭhāsavā* (influxes of views) is mentioned as the fourth.

the potency and sweeping influence of these influxes are also indicated by comparing them to floods (*ogha*).

In the context of latencies, influxes and floods, a complete re-orientation of sense-perception often becomes an arduous task requiring diligent practice. The Noble Eightfold Path in its transcendental aspect[46] provides the Noble Disciple with the necessary scheme of mental training whereby the process of accumulation of the five aggregates of grasping may be effectively checked, thus nullifying the influence of the aforesaid corrupting forces.

"Knowing and seeing the eye, monks, as it really is, knowing and seeing forms as they really are, knowing and seeing eye-consciousness as it really is, knowing and seeing eye-contact as it really is, and also knowing and seeing whatever feeling—pleasant, unpleasant or neither-unpleasant-nor-pleasant—that arises dependent on eye-contact, as it really is, one gets not attached to the eye, gets not attached to forms, gets not attached to eye-consciousness, gets not attached to eye-contact and gets not attached even to that feeling—pleasant, unpleasant or neither-unpleasant-nor-pleasant—that arises dependent on eye-contact. And for him as he abides unattached, unfettered, uninfatuated contemplating the peril (in eye, etc.), the five aggregates of grasping that would have arisen undergo effacement (*apacayaṃ gacchanti*). That craving which makes for re-becoming, which is accompanied by delight and lust, finding delight here and there, that too is abandoned in him. His bodily disturbances cease; his mental disturbances cease; his bodily afflictions cease; his mental afflictions cease; his bodily distresses cease; his mental distresses cease; and he experiences physical and mental happiness. Whatever view such a one has, that becomes for him Right View; whatever intention he has, that becomes for him Right Intention;

---

46. The distinction between the worldly and the transcendental aspects of the Eightfold Path is explained in the *Mahācattārīsaka Sutta* (M III 71ff.).

whatever effort he puts forth, that becomes for him Right Effort; whatever mindfulness he has, that becomes for him Right Mindfulness; and whatever concentration he has, that becomes for him Right Concentration. But his bodily actions and his verbal actions and his livelihood have already been purified earlier. So this Noble Eightfold Path comes to be perfected in him by development."—M III 288f., *Mahāsaḷāyatanika Sutta*.

The five aggregates of grasping which are said to be "compounded" or "concocted" (*saṅkhata*) are but accumulated sense-experience fermented by ignorance. Due to egotistic clinging in the form of "conceiving" (*maññanā*) sense-data become impregnated with this dynamic ferment and proliferation (*papañca*) follows. It is in view of this state of affairs that particular emphasis is laid on the necessity of viewing sense-data with detachment. The Buddha's advice to Bāhiya clearly indicates that this training has as much a philosophical as an ethical background. "Then, Bāhiya, thus must you train yourself: 'In the seen, there will be just the seen; in the heard just the heard; in the sensed, just the sensed; in the cognized, just the cognized.' That is how, Bāhiya, you must train yourself. Now when, Bāhiya, in the seen there will be to you just the seen; in the heard just the heard; in the sensed just the sensed; in the cognized just the cognized, then Bahiya, you will not be (reckoned) by it. And when, Bāhiya, you will not be (reckoned) by it, you will not be in it. And when, Bāhiya, you will not be in it, then, Bāhiya, you will not be 'here' nor 'there' nor 'midway-between.' This itself is the end of suffering"—Ud 8.

CHAPTER VIII

Suchness and the Suchlike-One

The principle underlying the twelve-linked formula of Dependent Arising is a law of nature that is universally applicable, whether one is dealing with the animate realm or the inanimate. It presents a dynamic view of all phenomena as they arise depending on causes, only to cease when these are removed.

This being, that comes to be;
With the arising of this, that arises.
This not being, that does not come to be;
With the cessation of this, that ceases.

The law is so integral that any two consecutive links of the formula would amply illustrate it. Hence we find the Buddha sometimes drawing a distinction between Dependent Arising (*paṭicca-samuppāda*) as such, and dependently arisen phenomena (*paṭiccasamuppannā dhammā*), well knowing the popular tendency to lose sight of the essentials by getting involved in details.

"Monks, I will teach you Dependent Arising and dependently arisen things … And what, monks, is Dependent Arising? From birth as condition, decay-and-death comes to be. Whether there be an arising of Tathāgatas or whether there be no such arising, this nature of things just stands, this causal status, this causal orderliness, the relatedness of this to that. Concerning that the Tathāgata is fully enlightened, that he fully understands. Fully enlightened, fully understanding, he declares it, teaches it, reveals it, sets it forth, manifests, explains, makes it plain, saying: 'Behold!'

"From birth as condition, decay-and-death comes to be; from becoming as condition birth … from ignorance as condition, formations come to be ... Thus, monks, that suchness therein—the invariability, the "not-otherwiseness," the relatedness of this to that—this, monks, is called Dependent Arising. And what, monks, are things dependently arisen? Decay-and-death is impermanent, compounded, dependently arisen, is of a nature to wither away, pass away, fade away and cease. So too is birth, becoming, grasping, craving, feeling, contact, six sense-spheres, name-and-form, consciousness, formations, ignorance. These also are impermanent, compounded, dependently arisen, are of a nature to wither away, pass away, fade away and cease. These, monks, are called things dependently arisen ..."—S II 25f.

"Suchness" (*tathatā*), "invariability" (*avitathatā*), "not-otherwise-ness" (*anaññathatā*) and "relatedness of this-to-that" (*idappaccayatā*: i.e., specific conditionality) are highly significant terms indicating the degree of importance attached by the Buddha to this law of Dependent Arising. The first three terms affirm the validity of the law. *Tathā*, it may be noted, is a word meaning "thus" or "such"—a rather "unassuming" type of expression carrying with it some nuances of detachment as well. As a correlate of *yathā*[47] ("in whatever way") *tathā* says little on its own, but for that very reason *tathatā* (suchness, thusness) becomes a fitting epithet for the principle of Dependent Arising. Here is a concept of truth shorn of all sectarian prejudice and pretension. A universal norm, true for all times irrespective of the arising of Tathāgatas to reveal and proclaim it, is indeed one that could rightly be called a "suchness."

The "relatedness of this-to-that" (*idappaccayatā*), which implies specific conditionality, is a term that brings out the essentially dependent and relative character of the phenomena through which the law finds expression. It explains, in particular, the significance of the pair-wise formulation, showing that in each pair, given the first

47. Cf. *Yathābhūtañāṇadassana*—"knowledge and vision of things as they are."

member, the second follows of necessity.[48] Phenomena have a tendency to manifest themselves as a flux—one conditioned phenomenon leading on to another. It is this dynamic aspect of the law that finds figurative expression in the following simile:

"The ocean, monks, when it swells, makes the great rivers swell; the great rivers when they swell, make their tributaries swell; these when they swell, make the mountain lakes swell; these when they swell, make the mountain tarns swell.

"Even so, monks, swelling ignorance makes formations swell, swelling formations make consciousness swell ... swelling birth makes decay-and-death swell.

"The ocean, monks, when it ebbs, makes the great rivers ebb; these make the tributaries ebb, these make the mountain lakes ebb, these make the mountain tarns ebb.

"Even so, monks, ebbing ignorance makes formations ebb, ebbing formations make consciousness ebb ... ebbing birth makes decay-and-death ebb"—S II 118f.

Thus the law holds good for both kinds of "flux"—that of water and that of psychological states. The process of tide and ebb is a tendency not only of water but of the saṃsāric individual as well.[49] The recognition of this process "as-it-is" marks a significant advance on the trends of animistic thought which, from pre-historic times, sought to explain phenomena in terms of essence, self or soul. It is all the more significant for its corollary that the entire process could be made to cease progressively by applying the proper means. Negatively put, the spiritual endeavour to end all suffering is a process of "starving" the conditions of their respective

---

48. A clearer enunciation of this is found at S II 79. It runs: "This being, that comes to be. With the arising of this, that arises. When there is ignorance (*avijjāya sati*) formations come to be (*saṅkhāra honti*)," etc.

49. Cf. *Kuto sarā nivattanti—kattha vaṭṭaṃ na vattati.* "Wherefrom do currents turn back—where whirls no more the whirlpool?"—S I 15.

"nutriments" (*āhāra*),[50] as indicated by the latter half of the formula of Dependent Arising. However, there are enough instances in the Pali Canon to show that it is quite legitimate to conceive this receding process positively too, as a progress in terms of wholesome mental states.

"Just as when, monks, on some hilltop when rain is falling in thick drops, that water, coursing according to the slope, fills the hillside clefts and chasms and gullies, these being filled up fill the tarns, these being filled up fill the lakes, these being filled up fill the little rivers, these being filled up fill the great rivers, and the great rivers being filled up fill the sea, the ocean—even so, monks, there is causal association of formations with ignorance, of consciousness with formations, of name-and-form with consciousness, of the sixfold sense-sphere with name-and-form, of contact with the sixfold sense-sphere, of feeling with contact, of craving with feeling, of grasping with craving, of becoming with grasping, of birth with becoming, of suffering with birth, of faith with suffering, of joy with faith, of rapture with joy, of serenity with rapture, of happiness with serenity, of concentration with happiness, of the knowledge-and-vision-of-things-as-they-really-are with concentration, of turning-away with the knowledge-and-vision-of-things-as-they-really-are, of dispassion with turning-away, of deliverance with dispassion, of knowledge about extinction (of influxes) with deliverance"—S II 32, *Upanisa Sutta*.

Instead of a "tide-and-ebb" we find in the above Sutta a "leading-onward" towards fullness or perfection, and it is this aspect of the Dhamma that finds expression in the epithet *opanayiko*. The famous simile of the relay-chariots in the *Rathavinīta Sutta* (M I 147ff.) depicts this "leading-onward" in a figurative way. A less figurative, but an equally effective expression of this fact, is found in the Buddha's words: "Thus, monks, mere phenomena flow into other phenomena, mere phenomena fill up (or perfect) other

50. See M I 260 ff., *Mahātaṇhāsaṅkhaya Sutta*.

phenomena in the process of passing from the "not-beyond" to the Beyond" (A V 3f.).[51]

There are some far-reaching conclusions flowing from a consideration of the law of Dependent Arising as a "suchness" and a specific-conditionality. As already mentioned (see above Ch. IV) this law has a wholesome effect on one's outlook in enabling one to avoid entanglement in speculative theories current in the world. In addition to it, the understanding of the flux within and without fosters an attitude of enlightened equanimity. One begins to look upon phenomena as impermanent (*anicca*) and void of essence (*suñña*) of any selfhood. What one imagined to be permanent now appears to be impermanent because one sees its arising and passing away. But a more astounding revelation comes in the form of the conviction that it is the very conceiving or egotistic imagining (*maññanā*) which gives rise to those phenomena or "things" (*dhammā*). To conceive is to conceive as a "thing," but that thing is, as it were, "still-born," for it cannot survive in a world where separation (*nānābhāvo*), privation (*vinābhāvo*) and otherwise-ness (*aññathābhāvo:* i.e., transformation) are the inexorable law. "Whatever thing they conceive of, *ipso facto* it turns otherwise; and that becomes false for him—the puerile delusive thing that it is."[52] Selfhood, which tries to sit pretty on that which is liable to disintegrate (*palokadhammaṃ*) is itself subject to the inexorable law of impermanence. In the face of this predicament one

---

51. See also *Mahācattārīsaka Sutta* (M III 76): "In one of Right View, Right Intention arises; in one of Right Intention, Right Speech arises; in one of Right Speech, Right Action arises; in one of Right Action, Right Livelihood arises; in one of Right Livelihood, Right Effort arises; in one of Right Effort, Right Mindfulness arises; in one of Right Mindfulness, Right Concentration arises; in one of Right Concentration, Right Knowledge arises; in one of Right Knowledge, Right Deliverance arises."

52. *Yena yena hi maññanti—tato taṃ hoti aññathā*
taṃ hi tassa musā hoti—mohadhammaṃ hi ittaraṃ—Sn 757; Ud 32.

craves, grasps and "becomes" yet another "thing"—which too yields to the same law of nature. "The world attached to becoming is becoming otherwise; subject to becoming, it yet delights in becoming. What it delights in, is a source of fear and what it fears is suffering."[53]

The process of becoming is thus shown to be perpetually going on within the mind of the saṃsāric individual[54] who identifies himself with sense-data under the influence of the proliferating tendencies towards craving, conceits and views. This identification is implied by the term *tammayatā* (lit. "of-that-ness") and one who resorts to it, is called *tammayo*—one who is "made-of-that" or is "of-that-(stuff)." Since the perpetual process of becoming in the psychological realm is necessarily followed by birth, decay-and-death, sorrow, lamentation grief and despair in every specific instance of short-lived identification, an insight into the law of Dependent Arising provides one with the key to the entire gamut of saṃsāric experience. One comes to understand the cycle of saṃsāric life by discovering its epicycle in the very structure of living experience. He is now convinced of the fact that it is craving that plays the villain in the drama of saṃsāric

---

53. *Aññathābhāvi bhavasatto loko—bhavapareto bhavamevābhinandati yadabhinandati taṃ bhayaṃ—yassa bhāyati tam dukkhaṃ*—Ud 31f.

54. "Just as, O monks, a monkey faring through the woods, through the great forest, catches hold of a bough, letting it go seizes another, even so, that which we call thought, mind, consciousness, that arises as one thing, ceases as another, both by night and by day. Herein, monks, the instructed noble disciple thoroughly and radically reflects (*sādhukaṃ yoniso manasikaroti*) on the Law of Dependent Arising itself: "This being, that comes to be, with the arising of this, that arises. This not being, that does not come to be; with the cessation of this, that ceases." That is to say, conditioned by ignorance formations come to be, conditioned by formations consciousness, conditioned by consciousness name-and-form ... Thus is the arising of this entire mass of suffering"—S II 95, *Assutavato.*

existence, bringing about re-becoming (*ponobhavika*) by delighting "now-here-now-there" (*tatratatrābhinandinī*).

Problems of existence—of life and death—which one had hitherto tried in vain to solve in the wider context of saṃsāric lives spread out in time and space, now find a solution in the timeless (*akāliko*) epicycle of saṃsāra revolving within the mind. Hence all. problems converge on the all-important issue of abandoning that craving which makes for re-becoming. By revealing the antecedents of craving, the law of Dependent Arising points to a technique whereby this tendency deeply ingrained in the ruts of our saṃsāric habits could be ferreted out of its sockets.[55] Ignorance has to be replaced by knowledge. In other words, the tendency to attend to the dependently arisen phenomena by imagining "things" in them, has to be overcome by training the mind to attend to the law of Dependent Arising instead. It might be recalled that each of the twelve links of the formula has been described as "impermanent, compounded, dependently arisen, of a nature to wither away, pass away, fade away and cease" (See above, Ch. VIII). The via media of training the mind to attend to the nature of things rather than to the things themselves may be called a rare type of psychotherapy introduced by the Buddha. It is a way of making the conditioned phenomena "fade away and cease" by penetrating into their cause. Thus, insight into the Noble Norm (*ariyo nayo*) of Dependent Arising implies a knowledge of the cause (*hetu*) as well as of the things causally arisen (*hetuppabhavā dhammā; hetusamuppannā dhammā*).[56] As the insight into the principle—"This being, that comes to be; with the arising of this, that arises. This not being, that does not come to be; with the cessation of this, that ceases"—goes

55. Note that the Second Noble Truth of the Arising of Suffering is sometimes defined simply as craving and sometimes as the Law of Dependent Arising (see e.g., S II 10; A I 177). The implication is that this formula explains the antecedents of craving, tracing it back to ignorance—its intellectual counterpart.

deeper and deeper into the fabric of the twelve-linked formula, a de-colouration or a fading-away ensues, with which one realizes the destruction of the very conditions (*paccaya*) forming the warp and woof of the formula in its direct and reverse order.[57]

The truth of impermanence is thus tested in the crucible of one's own experience—a panoramic view of the world arising and passing away as seen through one's own six sense-spheres.[58] The reference in the Udāna (1-3) to the Buddha's reflection on Dependent Arising in direct-order (*anuloma*), in reverse-order (*paṭiloma*) and in both direct- and reverse-order (*anuloma-paṭiloma*) soon after his Enlightenment has to be understood in this sense. This penetrative insight into the arising and cessation of phenomena dispels all doubts as to the speculative problems of absolute existence and non-existence, of unity and plurality, etc., and the mind is brought to rest in the "middle"

---

56. *Ye dhammā hetuppabhavā / tesaṃ hetuṃ tathāgato āha tesañca yo nirodho / evaṃvādī mahāsamaṇo*—Vin I 40f.

"Of things that arise from a cause
Their cause the Tathāgata has told
And also their cessation
Thus teaches the Great Recluse."

This stanza in which the venerable Assaji presented the quintessence of the Buddha's teaching to the wandering ascetic Sāriputta (later, the Chief Disciple, the "Foremost-in-Wisdom") is noteworthy in this connection. Both Sāriputta and Moggallāna attained the Fruit of Stream-winning on hearing it, as it aroused in them "the dustless, stainless Eye-of-Truth," i.e., the insight into the law of Dependent Arising.

According to the Dhammapada commentary (see *Aggāsavakavatthu*), both had already undergone a salutary mental crisis, when they got disgusted with the hill-top festival which they were witnessing. If the tradition is authentic, we may say that this preliminary insight into the backstage workings of the "magic-show" of consciousness had prepared their minds to a better reception of the Buddha's message.

though, paradoxically, it now rests on nothing. "Thingness" has completely faded away, so much so that craving finds "no-thing" to grasp at. Instead of an attempt at identification (*atammayatā*) impelled by craving, a detached contemplation of the norm of suchness (*tathatā*) sets in. With this emancipation of the mind, one's attitude towards the world with all its vicissitudes, becomes one of "Such-like-ness" (*tādita*)—of aloofness (*atammayatā*) and he deserves to be called the "Such-One" or the "Such-like One" (*tādī tādiso*). "That ardent one, who touched the destruction of birth by overcoming Māra—by vanquishing the Ender—that wise sage, the Such-like One, the Knower of the World, is unattached (*atammayo*) in regard to all phenomena."[59]

The attitude of the Such-like One reflects an extraordinary blend of qualities ranging from firmness and steadfastness to adaptability and resilience. To the worldling this appears as a paradox because he always associates the concept of firmness with some standpoint. Not to take up a standpoint is to vacillate, and hence he finds it difficult to conceive of a firmness apart from it. The Buddha, however, discovered that the truth is just the contrary.

I. "To the one attached (lit. one who is "supported,") there is wavering (or "dislodgement"), to the unattached one there is no wavering; wavering not being, there is calm; calm

---

57. *Yadā have pātubhavanti dhammā / ātāpino jhāyato brāhmaṇassa / athassa kaṃkhā vapayanti sabbā / yato khayaṃ paccayānaṃ avedi*—Ud 2.

"When phenomena manifest themselves to the perfect saint as he meditates ardently, then all his doubts are dispelled since he has understood the destruction of the conditions."

58. "In the six the world arose
In the six it holds concourse
On the six themselves depending
In the six it has its woes."—S I 41, *Loka Sutta*.

59. *Pasayha māraṃ abhibhuyya antakaṃ / Yo ca phusi jātikkhayaṃ padhānavā / So tādiso lokavidu sumedho / Sabbesu dhammesu atammayo muni*—A I 150.

being, there is no bending (i.e., inclination); bending not being, there is no coming-and-going; coming-and-going not being, there is no death-and-birth; there being no death-and-birth, there is neither a "here" nor a "there" nor any (position) "between-the-two." This itself is the end of suffering"—Ud 81; M III 266; S IV 59.

II. "The one unattached wavers not, but the one attached, who clings, does not transcend saṃsāra which is of the nature of "this-ness" and "otherwise-ness" (*itthabhāvaññathābhāvaṃ*). Knowing this peril, this great danger, in "supports" (*nissayesu*) let the monk fare along mindfully—resting on nothing, clinging to nothing"—Sn 752–3, *Dvayatānupassana Sutta*.

As the river-simile quoted above (see Ch. VI) illustrates, the worldling has the tendency to clutch at the "things" in the form of phenomena when he finds his "self" being swept away by the swift-flowing stream of nature. With cravings, conceits and views he tries to cling to and rest on the fleeting phenomena, only to be foiled in his attempts. Every attempt to salvage the "self" from the flux is followed by a definite series of psychological reactions. From the very moment of his identifying himself with the "thing" of his choice (i.e., *maññanā*) there sets in unsteadiness or wavering in the face of possible dislodgement. "Bending" or inclination is that blind reaching-out into the unknown future, prompted by craving or "thirst"—the "guide-in-becoming" (*bhavanetti*). The concepts of coming-and-going are relative to the standpoint already taken in the process of identification. A relationship having been thus established between one's present identity and a possible future state, there follows the corollary—"death-and-birth"—with its note of finality. With it, relative distinctions of a "here," a "there" and a "midway-between" also set in. The entire process, whether it be understood in the context of the epicycle of saṃsāra traceable to every moment of living experience or in the context of the larger cycle of saṃsāra[60] rolling in time and space, is a perpetual alternation between a "this-ness" and an "otherwise-ness" (*itthabhāvaññathābhāvaṃ*).

Now, the Such-like One, who sees the danger in resorting to "supports", which only give way underneath, grasps at nothing and clings to nothing. He has given up all standpoints (see above, *Kāḷakārāma Sutta*), and in so doing, has discovered a basis for firmness which never betrays. His is an unshakable deliverance of the mind (*akuppa-cetovimutti*) since he is free from attachment (*anurodha*) and repugnance (*virodha*) in the face of the worldly vicissitudes of "gain and loss, honour and dishonour, praise and blame, happiness and unhappiness" (see A IV 157). "In the case of a monk who is fully emancipated in mind, friends, though many forms cognizable through the eye may come within the range of the eye, they never obsess his mind; unalloyed is his mind, steady and become imperturbable and he sees its passing away. Though many sounds ... smells ... flavours ... tangibles ... ideas ... they never obsess his mind; unalloyed is his mind, steady and become imperturbable, and he sees its passing away ... " (A IV 404). The Buddha's declaration in the *Kāḷakārāma Sutta*—"Thus, monks, the Tathāgata, being Such-

---

60. A practical application of this principle to the problem of life and death comes in the *Channovāda Sutta* (M III 266, S IV 59). Here, the venerable Channa who was lying grievously ill contemplating suicide, was advised by the venerable Mahācunda to reflect on this particular aspect of the Buddha's teaching on detachment (i.e., passage I quoted above). As he declared with confidence to the venerable Sāriputta, his tempo of detachment had already reached a high degree. Though he committed suicide despite the latter's entreaties, we find the Buddha exonerating him on the ground that he died as an Arahant. The episode is rather revolting to "common sense" and it seems to touch a very delicate point in the doctrine. Nevertheless, if the deep philosophical implications of this short formula are appreciated, the episode would appear, at least, less revolting; for in one of those exceptional bids to out-do death, the venerable Channa had actually *overcome* death, though apparently he *succumbed* to it.

like in regard to all phenomena seen, heard, sensed and cognized, is 'such'"—is an allusion to this uninfluenced mind of the Emancipated One.

In spite of the fact that firmness is usually associated with rigidity, in a certain sense the Such-like One may be said to possess an adaptability and resilience, for which his epithet can easily find a place among its nuances. To revert to the river-simile again, the Such-like One has escaped from the swift-flowing stream by "letting-go" of both the "self" and the things seized as "supports" for the "self." This might sound like a paradox, but all that he has done is to attune himself to reality by getting rid of the illusion of self. As we saw above, it was this perverted notion that made him cling to the frail grasses on the riverbank in a bid to save his "self." The conceit of existence or "becoming" was the result of this clinging (*upādānapaccayā bhavo*) and all conceits of birth, decay and death were but relative to it. By penetrating into the truths of impermanence, suffering and not-self, the Such-like One has adapted himself to the worldly vicissitudes which are but manifestations of the above conceits. These vicissitudes do not "touch" him or affect him because he has already cut off all craving—"the guide-in-becoming" (*ucchinnabhavanettiko,* D I 46, *Brahmajāla Sutta*).

"'Steadied whereon the tides of conceit (*mānussavā*) no more occur in him and when the tides of conceit no more occur he is called a Hermit Stilled (*munisanto*).' So it was said. And with reference to what was this said? 'Am' is a conceit (*maññitaṃ*); 'I am this' is a conceit; 'I shall be' is a conceit; 'I shall not be' is a conceit; 'I shall be possessed of form' is a conceit; 'I shall be formless' is a conceit; 'I shall be percipient' is a conceit; 'I shall be non-percipient' is a conceit; 'I shall be neither-percipient-nor-non-percipient' is a conceit. Conceit is a disease, conceit is a cancer, conceit is a dart. It is with the surmounting of all conceits that he is called a Hermit Stilled. The Hermit who is Stilled neither is born nor ages nor dies; he is unshaken (*na kuppati*) and free from longing. He has none of that whereby he might be born. Not being born how shall he age? Not ageing how shall he die? Not dying how shall he be shaken? Being unshaken what shall he long for? So it was with reference to this that it was said: 'steadied whereon the tides of conceit no more occur in him and when the tides of conceit occur no more he is called a Hermit Stilled.'"[61]—M III 246, *Dhātuvibhaṅga Sutta*.

61. The translation (except for a few alterations) is from Venerable Ñāṇamoli.

CHAPTER IX
Essence of Concepts

Concepts play a prominent role in the "magic-show" of consciousness. Their influence is so pervasive that even the thinker in his quest for truth can hardly afford to dispense with them totally, however inadequate he finds them to be. In all transactions in mental life, concepts come in useful as "current-coin." The seeker after truth might doubt their provenance, but still he has to recognize their utility value—willy-nilly.

As we saw above, the Buddha discovered a Middle Path in regard to the problem of concepts when he distinguished between the law of Dependent Arising and the phenomena dependently arisen. Concepts, as dependently arisen phenomena, are illustrations of the law and hence their utility value was recognized. Yet, the Buddha pointed out that it is the insight into the law itself that is essential and that concepts, when once they have fully "illustrated" the law, must themselves fade away in that radiance of wisdom (*paññāpabha*)—having fulfilled their purpose.

This recognition of a higher purpose is an alchemy which transmutes the concept into a precursor of deliverance. It marks a remarkable advance on the extreme attitudes of dogmatism and cynicism or agnosticism and explains why the term *dhamma* ("thing," "phenomenon," "mind-object," "concept," "doctrine," "law," etc.) is such a generic term in Buddhism. Without clinging to the concept or trying to wriggle out of it, the Buddha penetrated deep into its character and revealed those strains in it that could be effectively utilized in one's quest for truth and freedom. Once he instructed the monks as to how they should reply to a series of questions that could be raised by wandering ascetics of other sects concerning the origin, behaviour and purpose of all "things."

"When thus questioned, monks, you may reply to those wandering ascetics as follows: "Rooted in desire (or interest), friends, are all things; born of attention are all things; arising from contact are all things; converging on feelings are all things; headed by concentration are all things; dominated by mindfulness are all things; surmountable by wisdom are all things; yielding deliverance as essence are all things; merging in the Deathless are all things; terminating in Nibbāna are all things." When thus questioned, monks, you may reply in this way to those wandering ascetics of other sects."—A V 106f.

Here the Buddha uses the generic term *dhamma*, which, for all practical purposes, may be rendered by "things." But that the reference is to thoughts and concepts is clearly revealed by the following catechism employed by the venerable Sāriputta to test the venerable Samiddhi's acquaintance with the above disquisition of the Buddha.

"With what as object, Samiddhi, do thoughts and concepts (*saṅkappa-vitakka*) arise in a man?"

"With name-and-form as object, venerable sir."

"But wherein, Samiddhi, do they assume diversity?"

"In the elements,[62] venerable sir."

"But whence, Samiddhi, do they arise?"

"They arise from contact, venerable sir "

"But on what, Samiddhi, do they converge?"

"They converge on feelings, venerable sir."

"But what, Samiddhi, is at their head?"

---

62. The eighteen elements: the elements of eye, of form, of eye-consciousness; the elements of ear, of sound, of ear-consciousness; the elements of nose, of odour, of nose-consciousness; the elements of tongue, of taste, of tongue-consciousness; the elements of body, of tangibles, of body-consciousness; the elements of mind, of ideas, of mind-consciousness. See S II 140ff.

"They are headed by concentration, venerable sir."
"But what is it, Samiddhi that dominates them?"
"They are dominated by mindfulness, venerable sir."
"But what, Samiddhi is their (point of) transcendence?"
"They are transcended by wisdom, venerable sir."
"But what is it, Samiddhi that forms their essence?"
"They have deliverance as their essence, venerable sir."
"But in what, Samiddhi do they get merged?"
"They get merged in the Deathless, venerable sir."

—A IV 385f.

From the Buddha's explanation regarding the origin of "things," their phenomenal character could easily be inferred, as stated in the pair of opening stanzas in the Dhammapada, "all things have mind as their forerunner, mind is their chief and they are mind-made.[63]" The worldling with his object-oriented world-view might find it difficult to appreciate the Buddha's words when he says that things are rooted in desire or interest (*chanda*), that they are born of attention (*manasikāra*) and that they arise from contact (*phassa*). By projecting his desires, the worldling has so alienated himself that he is prone to believe "word" and "meaning" to be eternally united in nature, even like the Divine Pair.[64] Radical reflection (*yoniso manasikāra*) as to the matrix of the concept would however reveal that "meaning"—as far as its meaning is concerned—is not very far from the psychological mainsprings whence arise all

63. *Mano pubbaṅgamā dhammā—manoseṭṭhā manomayā.*

64. See, for instance Kālidāsa: "I pay homage to the parents of the world, Pārvatī and Parameśvara, who are united like word and meaning (*vāgarthāviva saṃpṛktau*), so that it may conduce to a concord between word and meaning"—*Raghuvaṃśa* V 1. The contextual theory of meaning is an improvement on this popular view, though it has not fully explored the "psychological-context." The modern pragmatist also has rendered good service in breaking down some of the age-old myths concerning the relationship between word and meaning.

desires, interests, needs, purposes and designs (see above Ch. III). It is but the community of interests prompted by a measure of homosapient conceit that gives the concept its stamp of authority after infusing into it a particular set of meanings hammered out on the anvil of logic (*takkapariyāhata*). Once it comes out as a "finished product" one is apt to forget its compound and "synthetic" character, which it is the task of radical reflection to rediscover. In the matrix of the concept, "interest" isolates the "thing," the beam of attention magnifies it, while "contact" defines and circumscribes it.

To the extent concepts become "significant," they may be said to converge on feelings. The element of concentration that guides them and the power of mindfulness that dominates them are redeeming features of concepts, from the point of view of deliverance. The actual point of intersection, however, is "wisdom." Here, concepts are transcended, when penetrative wisdom which sees the rise-and-fall (*udayatthagāminī paññā*) intuits into the reverse and obverse of these "current-coins." They thus "expend" themselves yielding deliverance as their essence and get merged in the Deathless—reaching consummation in Nibbāna (see diagram).

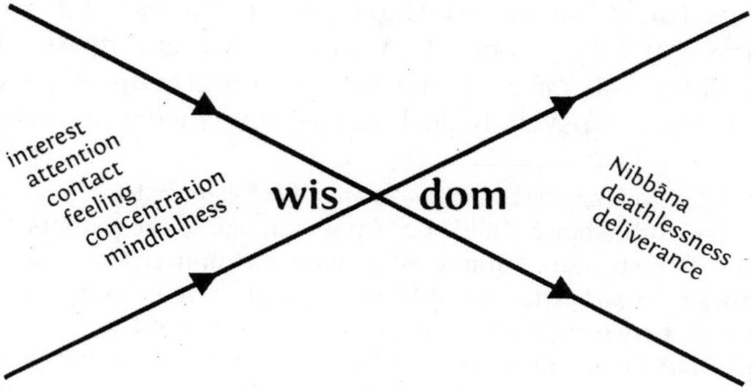

In rallying the concepts for the higher purpose of developing wisdom whereby concepts themselves are transcended, the Buddha has adopted a *via media* of a rare type. Concepts which make up the topsy-turvydom of saṃsāra are pressed into the service in order to develop the spiritual faculties—but always with adequate safeguards. This fact is well illustrated by the *Satipaṭṭhāna Sutta,* where each sub-section introducing a particular type of contemplation is followed by a paragraph-thematic in form—which neutralizes any errors of judgement that can easily arise from a too literal interpretation. For instance, the sub-section on the contemplation of the four postures is set out as follows:

"And further, O monks, when he is going, a monk understands: 'I am going'; when he is standing, he understands: 'I am standing;' when he is sitting, he understands: 'I am sitting'; when he is lying down, he understands: 'I am lying down'; or however his body is disposed, he understands accordingly.

"In this way he abides contemplating the body as a body in himself, or he abides contemplating the body as a body externally, or he abides contemplating the body as a body in himself and externally. Or else he abides contemplating the arising-nature in the body, or he abides contemplating the dissolving-nature in the body, or he abides contemplating the arising-and-dissolving nature in the body. Or else the mindfulness that 'There is a body' is established in him only to the extent necessary for just knowledge and remembrance, and he abides independent, not clinging to anything in the world,"—D II 292; M I 56f.

The dogmatist and the cynic, both of whom might go astray by interpreting too literally the words "I am going," I am standing," "I am sitting" and "I am lying down," should do well to note the significance of the practical hints given. Any undue emphasis on the "I am" is likely to give rise to an obsession with the idea of a self or an ego, and the cynic, for his part, is only too quick to notice here a contradiction with the teachings on *anattā* ("not-self"). But the mindfulness relating to body is not meant to be taken as an obsession with the body. Firstly, the provision for its application to others as well as to oneself is a way of universalising the principle involved in the practice, thereby ridding the mind of any tendency to get pre-occupied with the ego. Secondly, the contemplation of the arising-nature, the dissolving-nature, and the arising-and-dissolving nature of the body tends to keep away any notions of substantiality that may be associated with it, and furthermore prepares the mind for the final penetration of the concept of the body through wisdom. Lastly, the proviso that the awareness "There is a body" should be regarded merely as a means to an end—that its purpose is the sharpening of the spiritual faculties of mindfulness and wisdom—is a warning to those who "miss the wood for trees." A monk who keeps to the true spirit of the practice, therefore, is one who "abides independent, not clinging to anything in the world."

The constant awareness of its dependently arisen nature acts as a catalyst wherever the concept is utilized to subserve higher ends. The fact that it is only a "reckoning" (*saṅkha*) in the world is never lost sight of, and its composite nature is often analytically demonstrated. To this detached outlook, it mattered little whether the concept is that of a "house" or that of a "body." "Just as, friends, space equipped with timber and creepers and grass and clay comes to be reckoned as a "house," even so a space equipped with bones and sinews and flesh and skin comes to be reckoned as a 'form' (i.e., a 'body')"—M I 190, *Mahāhatthipadopama Sutta*.

Not only in regard to the contemplation of body (*kāyānupassanā*), but also in the case of the other three contemplations—i.e., those of feeling (*vedanānupassanā*), mind (*cittānupassanā*) and mind-objects (*dhammānupassanā*)—one is enjoined to observe the same practical hints. When in the case of these three it is stated that such mindfulness as "There are feelings," "There is a mind" or "There are mind-objects" is established in him only to the extent necessary for just knowledge and remembrance, it becomes evident that the Buddha had steered clear of the ontologist who is apt to treat such categories as absolute. According to the phenomenalistic approach of the Buddha, not only the "different types of feelings and mental states but the entire range of doctrinal categories summed up under the last section (i.e., "contemplation of mind-objects") has nothing in it that is worth "clinging to."[65] All of them can be subsumed under the term "concept" and that is to recognize their conditioned nature—the nature of arising-and-ceasing.

"Friends, when there is eye and there is form and there is eye-consciousness, it is possible that he will point out a designation of contact (*phassa-paññatti*). When there is a designation of contact, it is possible that he will point out a designation of feeling. When there is a designation of feeling, it is possible that he will point out a designation of perception. When there is a designation of perception, it is possible that he will point out a designation of thought (*vitakka-paññatti*). When there is a designation of thought, it is possible that he will point out a designation of obsession due to reckonings born of prolific perception (*papañcasaññāsaṅkhā-samudācaraṇa-paññatti*). When there is ear ... sound ... ear-consciousness ... When there is nose ... odour ... nose-consciousness ... When there is tongue ... flavour ... tongue-consciousness ... When there is body ... tangible ... body-consciousness ... When there is mind ... mind-object ... mind-consciousness ... a designation of obsession due to reckonings born of prolific perception."

"When, friends, there is no eye and there is no form and there is no eye-consciousness, it is impossible that he will point out a designation of contact. When there is no designation of contact, it is impossible that he will point out a designation of feeling. When there is no designation of feeling, it is impossible that he will point out a designation of perception. When there is no designation of perception, it is impossible that he will point out a designation of thought. When there is no designation of thought, it is impossible that he will point out a designation of obsession due to

65. Cf. *sabbe dhammā nālaṃ abhinivesāyā*, "nothing is worth clinging to"—M I 251, *Cūḷataṇhāsaṅkhaya Sutta*.

reckonings born of prolific perception. When there is no ear ... no sound ... no ear-consciousness ... When there is no mind and there is no mind-object and there is no mind-consciousness ... it is impossible that he will point out a designation of obsession due to reckonings born of prolific perception"—M I 112, *Madhupiṇḍika Sutta*.

It would indeed appear strange to us that in Buddhist psychology even contact and feeling—with which we are so intimate—are treated as "designations." We might feel that this is an intrusion of the "designation" into the jealously guarded recesses of the psyche. Yet this is not the case, for, in the very act of apperception, contacts and feelings are reckoned, evaluated, defined and designated on the basis of one's latencies (i.e., the aggregates).[66] Thus there is hardly any justification for regarding them as "the given," though we are accustomed to take them for granted. In other words, what we are wont to treat as "the given," turns out to be "synthetic" and "composite" (*saṅkhata*).

The concepts on which the "Four Foundations of Mindfulness" (*cattāro satipaṭṭhāna*) are "established," have nothing "essential" in them in any ontological sense. The entire structure is a mere network utilized for the development of mindfulness and wisdom. It is a net meant for "seeing through" and hence when penetrative wisdom is fully developed, consciousness soars untrammelled through the four-square meshes of the net.

"Monks, I will teach you the arising and going-down of the Four Foundations of Mindfulness. Listen attentively to it

---

66. *Yam-kho bhikkhu anuseti tam anumīyati yam anumīyati tena saṅkhaṃ gacchati. Rūpaṃ ce bhikkhu anuseti tam anumīyati yam anumīyati tena saṅkhaṃ gacchati: Vedanaṃ ce ... Saññaṃ ce ... Saṅkhāre ce... Viññāṇaṃ ce...*—S III 36f. "That which lies latent, monk, by that is one measured, and that by which one is measured, by that is one reckoned ..." "... If form, monk, lies latent, by that is one measured, that by which one is measured, by that is one reckoned. If feeling ... if perception ... if formations ... if consciousness ..."

... What, monks, is the arising of the body? With the arising of nutriment is the arising of the body; with the cessation of nutriment is the cessation of the body. With the arising of contact is the arising of feeling; with the cessation of contact is the cessation of feeling. With the arising of name-and-form is the arising of the mind; with the cessation of name-and-form is the cessation of the mind. With the arising of attention is the arising of mind-objects; with the cessation of attention is the cessation of mind-objects."—S V 184, *Samudayo Sutta.*

The catechism quoted at the beginning of this chapter reveals that the object dependent on which thoughts and concepts arise is "name-and-form." This comprehensive term, it may be recalled, is the "partner" of consciousness in the vortical-interplay (Ch. V). It is noteworthy that name-and-form is often associated with the idea of "entering into" or "getting entangled," while delusion is expressly called a net.

I. *Behold this world with all its gods*
Fancying a self where naught exists
Entering into name-and-form
It builds the conceit: "This is the Truth."

Sn 756, *Dvayatānupassana Sutta*

II. *Let one put wrath away, conceit abandon*
And get well beyond all fetters as well.
That one by name-and-form untrammelled
And possessionless—no pains befall.

Dhp 221, *Kodha Vagga* ("Anger")

III. *No fire like lust is there*
No grip so tight as hate
No net like crass delusion
No river like craving flows.

Dhp 251, *Mala Vagga* ("Impurities")

In the *Vaṅgīsa Sutta* of the *Suttanipāta* it is said that the venerable Nigrodhakappa "cut off the net of Maccu (an epithet of Māra)—the net so treacherously spread by the

Deceitful One" ("*acchiddā maccuno jālaṃ—tataṃ māyāvino daḷhaṃ*" Sn 357). The commentary identifies the net with craving, probably connecting it with the reference to craving in V 355.

"He cut off craving for this name-and-form"—so said the Lord.

"Kaṇha's[67] stream which had lain so long ..."

It is more likely, however, that the "net of Maccu" here referred to is name-and-form. Delusion is compared to a net[68] in the above verse of the *Dhammapada,* and moreover, the image usually associated with craving, which is always dynamic, is either a river (*nadi*) or a stream (*sota*) as in the two verses quoted above.

Owing to craving, consciousness finds itself enmeshed in name-and-form—its object (*ārammaṇa*). All speculative views based on sense-experience, however "logical" they may appear, are but cobwebs on the net. Hence, when the dogmatic philosopher clings to the theory he has spun out from his limited viewpoint and asserts: "I know, I see, 'tis verily so" (see above *Kāḷakārāma Sutta*), all that he sees, according to the Buddha, is the net of name-and-form:

"Some arrive at purity through dogmatic views, saying: "I know, I see, it is verily so." Even if he had seen, what difference does it make to him? Having by-passed the truth, it is by another (alien) means that they proclaim purity."

"A seeing man will see name-and-form and having seen, he will know those alone, verily let him see much or less; yet the experts do not speak of purity thereby"—Sn 908–9, *Mahāviyūha Sutta.*

All objects of the six senses lure into the net of name-and-form—craving being the decoy.[69] Worldly consciousness always finds itself glued to this or that object, which tends to

67. Kaṇha: "Blackie," an epithet of Māra.

68. Note that the speculative views representative of delusion are often compared to nets (*diṭṭhijāla*)— See D I 46, *Brahmajāla Sutta.*

becloud its vision of reality. These objects, forming the meshes of the net, have a simulating nature about them (see above: "double-bind"), which makes it difficult for one to thrust them out of the whole scheme of conscious life. They cannot be wished away, for they are there so long as the senses are there. Greed, hatred and delusion, which those objects as signs signify, are not abandoned verbally or physically, but by wisdom: "What, monks, are those things that are abandoned neither by body nor by word but by continually seeing with wisdom? Greed ... hatred ... delusion ... anger ... etc." (A V 39f). It is, therefore, when consciousness is weaned away from the tendency to get enmeshed in the net of name-and-form that the essence of the concept—"Deliverance—is attained Then one will be gazing not at the net but through it, not at the "things" but at the nature of "things." And it will be a gaze that is neither attentive, nor non-attentive, neither conscious nor non-conscious, neither fixed nor not-fixed—a gaze that knows no horizon.

---

69. Craving is called an "ensnarer" (*jālinī*—i.e., "one having a net") in the following verse of the Dhammapada (V 180):

Yassa jālinī visattikā / taṇhā natthi kuhiñci netave
tam buddhaṃ anantagocaraṃ / apadaṃ kena padena nessatha

"By what track can you lead that Awakened One who is trackless and to whom there is not that agglutinative ensnarer, "Craving"—to lead anywhere."

Another epithet of craving that can be related to this idea is *sibbanī*: "seamstress" (Sn 1040; A III 399f).

CHAPTER X

Non-Manifestative Consciousness

"Consciousness which is non-manifestative[70]—endless, lustrous on all sides,

Here it is that earth and water—fire and air no footing find;

Here, again, are long and short—fine and coarse—pleasant and unpleasant

And name-and-form—are cut off without exception.

When consciousness comes to cease—all these are held in check herein."

D I 223 *Kevaḍḍha Sutta.*

The illusory nature attributed to consciousness by the Buddha is, in a sense, a recognition of its reflexive character. Like a mirror (see above, Ch. VI) it reflects the five aggregates, the fifth of which is consciousness itself. This, indeed, is a magical illusion. Consciousness, when it reflects itself, reflects as "self-consciousness," and in fact all consciousness in the normal sense is self-consciousness. There is a curious duplicity involved, a veritable paradox. When one "identifies" oneself as reflected in the mirror of consciousness, saying: "I am" or "Here I am," one has already taken for granted a duality, though unwittingly. Already, a gap is created as a split in experience, and consequently there sets in the possibility of "measuring" as conceit (*māna*). Stated otherwise, it is a

---

70. Some aspects of this subject have already been discussed in my earlier works: *Concept and Reality in Early Buddhist Thought* (Kandy: Buddhist Publication Society, 1971); *Saṃyutta Nikāya: An Anthology, Part II* (Wheel Nos. 183/185); *Ideal Solitude: An Exposition of the Bhaddekaratta Sutta* (Wheel No. 183).

dependence, or rather, an inter-dependence (see above, Ch. V). Just as much as one gazing at a mirror becomes aware not only of his form but also of the contact, feeling, perception, intention and attention pertaining thereto, in becoming self-conscious, too one is aware of a similar set of "objects" which are collectively called "name-and-form."

As in any magic-show, here too an important part is played by "form" (*rūpa*). That inertia peculiar to form provides the basis for the most elementary judgement involved in the life of all organisms, namely, the dichotomy of existence and non-existence. "Seeing destruction and existence in material objects, a person arrives at a resolution in the world"—("*rūpesu disvā vibhavaṃ bhavañca—vinicchayaṃ kurute jantu loke*"—Sn 867, *Kalahavivāda Sutta*). Material objects appear to persist for some period before they get destroyed and in them the law of impermanence has found a camouflage. It is possible that the perverted notion (*vipallāsa*) of permanence is radically traceable to a misjudgement in regard to material objects whereby the ever-present process of change was overlooked and the two extreme views of absolute existence and absolute non-existence came to be asserted.

But this is just one strand in the "tangle" of saṃsāric life forming the "double-bind" (see Ch. V). There is another. It is the notion of sense-reaction or resistance (*paṭigha*), which represents the polar opposite of the inertia associated with the perception-of-form (*rūpasaññā*). It manifests itself as contact, feeling, perception, intention and attention comprising "name" in "name-and-form." The actual situation called sense-contact arises when both "name" and "form" collaborate. "Depending on 'name' and 'form' arise contacts" ("*nāmañca rūpañca paṭicca phassa*"—Sn 872). Hence when "form" ceases to exist, contacts cease to function ("*rūpe vibhūte na phusanti phassā*"—ibid.). The problem, then, boils down to this: "To one endowed in which manner does form cease to exist?" ("*kathaṃ sametassa vibhūti rūpaṃ*"—ibid., V 873).

The reply to this question comes in the form of a paradox: "Neither is he percipient of normal perception, nor is he one of abnormal perception. He is not non-percipient nor has he put an end to perception. It is to one who is thus constituted that form ceases to function, for reckonings characterised by conceptual prolificity have perception as their source."[71]

Here we have an extraordinary level of perception which has fully extricated itself from the obsession of form, so basic to the structure of perception. The negative formulation indicates that the transcendence is not by temporary or permanent suppression of perception. Rather, it suggests a case of seeing *through* perception so that if anyone had enquired whether he was conscious of any sense-data or whether he was unconscious or non-conscious or completely without consciousness at the time he was in this level of perception, he would have replied in the negative. Once, when the Buddha was staying in the chaff-house at Ātuma, there was a torrential downpour of rain accompanied by lightning and thunder, in the course of which two farmers and four bulls at the chaff-house were struck down by lightning. A big crowd of people had gathered at the place of accident and the Buddha, coming out of the chaff-house, was pacing up and down by its gate. A man from that crowd came up to him and saluted him and then this dialogue followed:

"Why, friend, has this big crowd gathered here?"

"Just now, lord, when it was raining in torrents with flashes of lightning and peals of thunder, two farmers—

---

71. *Na saññasaññī na visaññasaññī no pi asaññī na vibhūtasaññī evaṃ sametassa vibhoti rūpaṃ saññānidānā hi papañcasaṅkhā*—Sn 874. A free translation would require commoner expressions like "conscious" and "unconscious." All along, it is a question of perception (*saññā*) but since apperception is implied by the word *saññī*, it conveys the sense of being "conscious" of something. This rendering is also used below.

brothers—and four bulls were killed. That is why this big crowd has gathered. But where were you, lord?"

"I was here itself, friend."

"Why, lord, didn't you see (what happened)?"

"No friend, I did not see."

"But, lord, didn't you hear the sound?"

"No, friend, I did not hear the sound."

"Why, lord, were you asleep (at the time)?"

"No, friend, I was not sleeping."

"Why, lord, were you conscious (at the moment)?"

"Yes, friend."

"So then, lord, you being conscious (*saññī samāno*) and awake neither saw nor heard anything though it was raining in torrents with flashes of lightning and peals of thunder!"

"That is so, friend."

D II 131f., *Mahāparinibbāna Sutta*

This dialogue might not appear so strange to you since you have had a foretaste of it at the "magic-show." Nevertheless, that state of concentration which partakes of such a paradoxical character did appear strange not only to "a-man-from-the-crowd" but even to monks and nuns who were not yet Arahants. Time and again we find them enquiring from the Buddha or from the senior disciples about the possibility and nature of such a concentration.[72] Once the venerable Ānanda put the following question to the Buddha:

"Could there be, lord, for a monk such an attainment of concentration wherein he will not be conscious of earth in earth (*na paṭhavismiṃ paṭhavisaññī*), nor of water in water, nor of fire in fire, nor of air in air, nor will he be conscious of the sphere of infinity of space in the sphere of infinity of space, nor of the sphere of infinity of consciousness in the sphere of infinity of consciousness, nor of the sphere of nothingness in the sphere of nothingness, nor of the sphere of neither-perception-nor-non-perception in the sphere of

72. A IV 426ff., V 7f., 318ff., 322ff., 353ff.

neither-perception-nor-non-perception, nor will he be conscious of a 'this world' in this world, nor of a 'world beyond' in a world beyond—and yet he will be conscious?"

The Buddha replies that there could be such a state of concentration for a monk and on being questioned as to how it is possible, he explains:

"Herein, Ānanda, a monk is thus conscious (*evaṃsaññi*): 'This is peace, this is excellent, namely, the calming down of all formations, relinquishment of all assets (or substrata, *upadhi*), destruction of craving, detachment, cessation, Nibbāna.' It is thus, Ānanda, that there could be for a monk such an attainment of concentration ...—A V 7f.

From this explanation it appears that perception is not completely rescinded here, only it has now discovered some kind of quasi-object worth attending to, instead of the usual objects such as earth, water, fire and air. It is none other than the cessation aspect of Dependent Arising, in the contemplation of which all formations that go to compound "things" are completely calmed down. Consequently, all assets get liquidated, craving loses its sanction and supreme detachment, as the transcendental experience of the cessation of all existence, is thereby realized even here and now. That this is a dynamic vision in which all percepts and concepts are deprived of their object-status is revealed by the following explanation given by the venerable Sāriputta when the venerable Ānanda put the self-same question to him:

"'Cessation of becoming is Nibbāna, cessation of becoming is Nibbāna': thus, friend, one perception arises in me, another perception fades out in me. Just as, friend, when a faggot-fire is blazing, one flame arises and another flame fades out, even so, friend, one perception arises in me: 'Cessation of becoming is Nibbāna' and another perception fades out in me: 'Cessation of becoming is Nibbāna.' At that time, friend, I was conscious of this: 'Cessation of becoming is Nibbāna.'"—A V 9f.

Here, then, is a consciousness of the very cessation of consciousness.[73] Though well nigh a contradiction, it is yet a possibility because of the reflexive character of consciousness. Instead of a consciousness of objects, here we have a consciousness which is without an object or support.[74] Whereas, under normal circumstances, consciousness "mirrors" or manifests something, in this concentration it is "non-manifestative." It is as though, in a moment of detached contemplation, one has become aware of a raging fire, where formerly one had noticed only stock-piles of fire-wood.

"Form, monks, is on fire; feeling is on fire; perception is on fire; formations are on fire; consciousness is on fire.

"Thus seeing, monks, the instructed noble disciple gets disgusted with form; gets disgusted with feeling; gets disgusted with perception; gets disgusted with formations; gets disgusted with consciousness. Being disgusted, he becomes dispassionate; through dispassion he is released; and in release there comes the knowledge of release. Extinct is birth, lived out is the holy-life, done is the task, and he understands: 'There is nothing beyond this for (a designation of) the conditions of this existence'"—S III 71, *Āditta Sutta*.

That there is a radical change of attitude resulting in a shift of focus from fuel to fire or from nutriment to its significance is well illustrated by the Buddha's discourse to the venerable Sandha on this subject. There he draws a distinction between the musing of an unruly horse and that of a thoroughbred. An unruly horse tethered to the trough does not think: "What step of training will the trainer make me undergo today? How best should I respond to him?" Instead, it goes on musing: "Fodder, fodder." An excellent thoroughbred horse, on the other hand, does not muse: "Fodder, fodder" even though it is tethered to the trough, but goes on musing: "What step of training will the trainer make

---

73. Cf. (i) *ṭhitaṃ cittaṃ vippamuttaṃ vayañcassānupassati*—A III 379. "Mind is firm and well released—he sees its passing-away."
(ii) "When consciousness comes to cease"—*viññāṇassa nirodhena* (see verse at the head of this chapter).

74. I.e., *anārammaṇaṃ*. It is also called "unestablished" (*appatiṭṭhaṃ*) and "not-continuing" (*appavattaṃ*). See below.

me undergo today? How best should I respond to him?" Such a horse considers it as a debt, a bond, a misfortune or bad luck, to get whipped. With this simile the Buddha illustrates the difference between the worldly musing of an untrained man and the transcendental musing of "a good thoroughbred-of-a-man." The former, gone into solitude, does not understand as it really is the stepping-out from sensuous lust, ill-will, sloth and torpor, restlessness-and-worry, and doubt, and dwells with a mind obsessed with those five hindrances, brooding on them. And he muses on earth, water, fire, air, sphere of infinity of space, sphere of infinity of consciousness, sphere of nothingness, sphere of neither-perception-nor-non-perception; he muses dependent on this world, on the world beyond, on whatever is seen, heard, sensed, cognized, attained, sought after and traversed by the mind-dependent on all that he muses. But a good thoroughbred-of-a-man gone into solitude, does not dwell obsessed with the hindrances, brooding on them, as he understands the "stepping-out" from them. And he does not muse dependent on earth, water, fire, air and other "objects" above mentioned. "Nevertheless," it is said, "he does muse" ("*jhāyati ca pana*"). This musing which is not dependent on any object is said to be so strange that even gods and Brahmas from afar bow down saying:

We worship thee, thou thoroughbred of men,
We worship thee, most excellent of men.
For what it is whereon depending thou
Art musing—that we cannot comprehend.[75]

A V 323ff.

"Objects" play no part in this "perception" precisely for the reason that the "subject" is missing. This experience of

---

75. Cf. *avitakka-samādhi*—"thought-less concentration" (Ud 71); *avitakka jhāyi*—"one who meditates thoughtless" (S I 126); *jhāyati anupādāno*—"meditates fuel-less or without clinging" (Th 846–861); *avitakkaṃ samāpanno*—"one who has attained to the thoughtless concentration" (Th 999).

the cessation of existence (*bhavanirodho*), which is none other than "Nibbāna here-and-now," is the outcome of the eradication of the conceit "I am."[76] It is the element of egotistic measuring or reckoning present in a perceptual situation that results in full-fledged concepts. "What, monks, is the result of perception? Monks, I say that perception has usage as its result. As one perceives so one expresses it, saying: 'I was of such a perception (i.e., "thus conscious").'"[77] "Reckonings characterised by conceptual proliferation have perception as their source" (see above, Sn 874). When name-and-form, which stands in the relation of "object" (*ārammaṇa*) to consciousness is transcended, the latter loses its point of reference—its foothold. Hence earth, water, fire and air, together with such relative distinctions as long and short, subtle and gross, pleasant and unpleasant "find no footing" in that non-manifestative consciousness. The fecundity of concepts which manifests itself in normal perception as the "essence" or "substance," is thereby destroyed.

"Consciousness which is non-manifestative, infinite and lustrous all round: it does not partake of the solidity of earth, the cohesiveness of water, the hotness of fire, the movement of air, the creaturehood of creatures, the devahood of devas, the Pajāpatihood of Pajāpati, the Brahmāhood of Brahmā, the radiance of the Radiant Ones, the lustre of the Lustrous Ones, the Vehapphalahood of the Vehapphala Brahmas, the Overlordship of the Overlord and the allness of the all."[78]—M I 329f., *Brahmanimantanika Sutta*.

Having lost their fecundity in the emancipated mind, concepts do not lend themselves to proliferation (*papañca*). The emancipated one, who has realized the voidness of concepts through higher knowledge, no longer entertains egotistic imaginings based on them.

---

76. See A IV 358.

77. *Vohāravepakkāhaṃ bhikkhave saññaṃ vadāmi yathā yathā naṃ sañjanati tathā tathā voharati evaṃsaññī ahosin-ti*, A III 413.

"And the Tathāgata, too, monks, who is an Arahant, Fully Enlightened, understands earth as earth through higher knowledge: knowing earth as earth through higher knowledge, he does not conceive earth to be earth; he does not conceive: 'on the earth;' he does not conceive: 'from the earth;' he does not conceive: 'earth is mine;' he does not delight in earth. What is the reason for this? I say, it is because it has been well comprehended by him"—M I 5f., *Mūlapariyāya Sutta.*

As the *Kāḷakārāma Sutta* puts it, the Tathāgata does not conceive of a visible thing as apart from sight and entertains no conceits of a "thing-worth-seeing" or of a seer. This is the result of the conviction gained through his transcendental experience of the extinction of all phenomena in that non-manifestative consciousness.

When consciousness is not arrested by any object at the point of focus, it penetrates through the net of name-and-form out into an infinitude, and "viewpoints" give place to an all. encompassing vision. In this respect, it is described as "lustrous-all-round" (*sabbatopabham*), and the lustre is wisdom itself.[79] The illumination brings about a "fading away" (*vịrāga*) of all objects which earlier appeared to be "significant" due to the bewitching gleam of sense-

---

78. *Sabbassa sabbattena ananubhūtaṃ:* "Consciousness which does not partake of the allness of the all." Cf. "Monks, I will teach you the "all." Listen well ... What, monks, is the "all"? Eye and forms; ear and sounds; nose and smells; tongue and tastes; body and tangibles; mind and ideas. This, monks, is called the "all." "Whoever, monks, should say: 'Rejecting this "all" I will point out another "all"—it will only be a vain boast on his part, and when questioned, he will not be able to make good his boast. Furthermore, he will come to an ill pass. Why so? Because, monks, it is beyond his power to do so"—S IV 15.

79. Cf. "Monks, there are these four lustres (*pabhā*). What are the four? The lustre of the moon, the lustre of the sun, the lustre of fire, the lustre of wisdom ... Monks, among these four, the lustre of wisdom (*paññāpabhā*) is indeed the most excellent"—A II 139f.

"No lustre like unto that of wisdom"—S I 6.

consciousness. Consequently, this experience is sometimes referred to as "the cessation of the six sense-spheres" (*saḷāyatananirodha*).

"Therefore, monks, that sphere should be known wherein the eye ceases and the perception of form fades away; the ear ceases and the perception of sounds fades away; the nose ceases and the perception of smells fades away; the tongue ceases and the perception of tastes fades away; the body ceases and the perception of tangibles fades away; the mind ceases and the perception of ideas fades away—that sphere should be known, that sphere should be known."—S IV 98, *Lokakāmaguṇa* (2).

The monks who referred this brief utterance of the Buddha to the venerable Ānanda for explanation were told that it concerns the cessation of the six sense-spheres. Just as much as the cessation of consciousness is called "non-manifestative consciousness" in so far as it is yet a level of experience,[80] the cessation of the six sense-spheres is also described as a sphere (*āyatana*).

"There is, monks, that sphere wherein there is neither earth, nor water, nor fire, nor air; wherein is neither the sphere of infinity of space, nor that of infinity of consciousness, nor that of nothingness, nor that of neither-perception-nor-non-perception; wherein there is neither this world nor a world beyond, nor moon and sun. There, monks, I declare, is no coming, no going, no stopping, no passing-away and no arising. It is not established (*appatiṭṭhaṃ*), it continues not (*appavattaṃ*), it has no object (*anārammaṇaṃ*). This indeed is the end of suffering"—Ud 80.

The world of sense-experience where laws of relativity dominate is thus transcended in a "sphere" which is not somewhere in outer space but within this very fathom-long

---

80. Cf. … *chando ca vūpasanto hoti vitakko ca vūpasanto hoti saññā ca vūpasantā honti tappaccayāpi vedayitāni*—S V 13. "Desire is appeased, thought is appeased, perceptions are appeased, owing to that also there is an experience."

body.[81] Together with those sense-objects which appear to be concrete such as earth, water, fire, air, sun and moon, such abstract notions associated with them as "coming," "going," "stopping," "passing-away" and "arising," also fade away. Sights, sounds, smells, tastes, touches and ideas—all of which are "signs" (see Ch. III)—have now lost their "significance." They no longer signify "things," for lust, hatred and delusion are extinct in the emancipated one. All that his "Signless Deliverance of the Mind" (*animitta cetovimutti*—see M I 298, *Mahāvedalla Sutta*) now signifies is the very absence of lust, hatred and delusion in him which, in effect, is the knowledge of Nibbāna (*aññā*)—the cessation of all birth and becoming and of all formations that breed manifold suffering.

"Monks, there is a not-born, a not-become, a not-made, a not-compounded. Monks, if that not-born, not-become, not-made, not-compounded were not, there would be no stepping out here from what is born, become, made, compounded. But since, monks, there is a not-born, a not-become, a not-made, a not-compounded, therefore, there is a stepping-out from what is born, become, made and compounded"[82]—Ud 80f.

The world enfettered to delusion
Feigns a promising mien
The fool to his assets bound
Sees only darkness around
It looks as though it would last
But to him who sees there's naught.

Ud 79.

Sights, sounds, smells, tastes, touches, ideas,
All what they deem desirable—charming, pleasing things
Of which they claim: "it is"—as far as their claim extends

---

81. Cf. "... It is in this very fathom-long physical frame with its perceptions and mind that, I declare, lies the world and the arising of the world and the cessation of the world and the path leading to the cessation of the world"— S I 62, *Rohitassa Sutta*.

The world with its gods is agreed that these are pleasant things
And wherein they surcease—"That's unpleasant indeed' say they.
As bliss the Noble Ones have seen the curb on self-hood bias.
Behold! In contrast is their vision with that of the entire world.
What others spoke of in terms of bliss, that as woe the saints declared.
What others spoke of in terms of woe, that as bliss the saints have known.
Behold! A Norm so hard to grasp—baffled herein are ignorant ones.
Murk it is to those enveloped, as darkness unto the undiscerning,
But to the Good wide open it is, as light is unto those discerning.

---

82. In a psychological sense, a design could be "unmade" or "dissolved" by shifting one's attention to its components. Even so, "what is born" (*jātaṃ*), "become" (*bhūtaṃ*), "made" (*kataṃ*) and "compounded" (*saṅkhataṃ*) is transformed into a "not-born," "not-become," "not-made" and "not-compounded" state by a penetrative insight into its causes and conditions. All "designs" involved in the magic-show of consciousness, which are but dependently arisen, also cease when ignorance and craving are eradicated.

The above epithets of Nibbāna are therefore psychological, and not metaphysical, in their import. Where there is no "putting-together." there is no "falling-apart." Hence Nibbāna is also called *apalokitaṃ*—the "Non-disintegrating." It is unfortunate that many scholars, both Eastern and Western, have interpreted metaphysically the two passages from the Udāna quoted here, bringing out conclusions which are hardly in keeping with the teachings on *Anattā*. The widespread tendency is to see in these two passages a reference to some mysterious, nondescript realm in a different dimension of existence, though the Buddha was positive that all existence is subject to the law of impermanence.

So near, and yet they know not—Fools! Unskilled in the
Norm.
By those who are given to lust for becoming,
By those who are swept by the current of becoming,
By those who have slipped into Māra's realm,
Not easily comprehended is this Norm.
Who else but the Noble Ones deserve
To waken fully unto that state
By knowing which, being influx-free,
Tranquil Nibbāna they attain.

Sn 759–765, *Dvayatānupassana Sutta.*

CHAPTER XI

Peace is Bliss in Nibbāna—An Epilogue

Lead me from untruth to truth!
Lead me from darkness to light!
Lead me from death to deathlessness!

Such was the yearning of the Indian mind. It was a yearning in sympathy with the highest aspirations of mankind. The *Kāḷakārāma Sutta*, when understood in the light of the salient teachings of the Buddha, would go a long way in showing us how this yearning could be fulfilled.

There is, however, a radical departure in Buddhism in regard to the approach to these problems of truth, light and deathlessness. Truth, which is the key to the riddle of existence, was hitherto believed to be in the custody of a Godhead. Light, which dispels the gloom of the spirit, could be propitiated—it was thought—only in a mystic absorption with that Godhead. Immortality, which solves the problem of death—the inexorable tragedy of all living beings—was supposed to have been secured only in a different dimension of existence where the immortal gods (*amara*) eternally revel in their ambrosia (*amrita*).

In contradistinction to this popular psychology, the naiveté of which the metaphysicians tried in vain to conceal, comes the message of the Buddha. He discovered truth where one least expected to find it. Existence and its cessation, the problem and its solution, were found interwoven in a tangle at the very vortex of all existence—if only one could disentangle it! And this he successfully did and also revealed to humanity the way of setting about it. Truth, according to him, is in no one's custody and has no esoterism or mysticism associated with it. It is a question of "seeing things as they are" and once the necessary clarity of vision is developed, one could see it in all its lucidity and limpidity in the very structure of all phenomena. Dhamma as truth, invites one to "come-and-see" (*ehipassiko*).

"Just as if there were a lake in a mountain-recess, clear, limpid and unturbid so that a man with good eyes standing there on the bank saw shells, gravel and pebbles and also shoals of fish swimming about and resting, who might think: 'There is this lake, clear, limpid and unturbid and there are these shells, gravel and pebbles and also shoals of fish swimming about and resting,' so too, monks, a monk understands, as it really is 'This is suffering;' he understands as it really is: 'This is the arising of suffering;' ... This is the cessation of suffering;' ... This is the path leading to the cessation of suffering.' He understands as they really are: 'These are influxes;' he understands as it really is: 'This is the arising of influxes;' ... 'This is the cessation of influxes;' ... This is the path leading to the cessation of influxes.' And the mind of him who knows and sees thus is released from the influxes of sense-desires, from the influxes of becoming, from the influxes of ignorance. In release there arises the knowledge of release and he understands: Extinct is birth, lived out is the holy life, done is the task; there is nothing beyond this for (a designation of) the conditions of this existence" M I 279f., *Mahā Assapura Sutta*.

The darkness that beclouds the clarity of vision in our mental life was traced by the Buddha to the delusion of a "self." The delusion as "the point-of-view" (see above Ch. VI) created a background of ignorance in order to perpetuate itself. The mind became committed and limited due to ignorance and craving. Here is a case of "possession" giving rise to a "prepossession," an "acquisition" resulting in a "privation." The knowledge amassed by the six sense-spheres functioning within the narrow confines staked out for them by the ego, was thus found to be tantamount to an "ignorance." There was the inevitable dichotomy of an "internal" and an "external" sense-base and consciousness was cramped up between a "here" and a "there"(see Ch. V). The problem of illumination, therefore, was not dependent on any union or absorption with a Godhead, which is equivalent to merging one darkness ("self") in another darkness ("Self"). Only the "self-created" artificial confines had to be broken down with a penetrative flash of wisdom in order that consciousness may develop its capacity to be infinite and all-lustrous. And the discovery that this capacity is already there in the mind (if only one could develop it!) comes as an unexpected revelation to mankind.

"This mind, monks, is luminous, but it is defiled by extraneous defilements. That the uninstructed ordinary man does not understand as it is. Therefore there is no mind-development for the uninstructed ordinary man, I declare.

"This mind, monks, is luminous, and it is released from extraneous defilements. That the instructed noble disciple understands as it is. Therefore there is mind-development for the instructed noble disciple, I declare"—A I 10.

The Buddha realized that "birth" and "death" are inseparable corollaries of the conceit of existence. The law of impermanence, which holds sway even in heavenly realms, would militate against any notion of immortal existence. Besides, the quest for immortal existence was only a symptom of the deep-seated fear of death. If only this obsessional fear could be removed the problem would be no more. Hence he advanced a novel type of solution to the problem of life and death. He pointed out that although immortal existence is impossible, one could still experience "ambrosial" deathlessness—and that even here and now."[83] One had to recognize fully the truths of impermanence, suffering and not-self whereby "existence," on which both "birth" and "death" depended, is made to cease. The remedy, it would appear, was somewhat on "homoeopathic" lines though the "dose" of impermanence to be administered was by no means minute. The approach was so radical that it even entailed the strange paradox that if the reflection on death is systematically well developed it would get merged in the Deathless (*amatogadhā,* A V 105)! Thus instead of attempting to "stifle" death artificially by heavenly ambrosia, the Buddha saw to it that death died a *natural* death in a sphere of transcendental experience of a Deathless attainable in this very "mortal world."

"That destruction (of craving), that detachment, that excellent (ambrosial) deathlessness which the Sakyan Sage attained being concentrated—there is nothing comparable to that Dhamma ...—Sn 225, *Ratana Sutta.*[84]

The Buddha's approach—it may be repeated—was so radical that it even dispensed with the supplicating attitude behind the words "Lead me" in the yearning cited above. The Dhamma as the suchness of phenomena (see Ch. VIII) had the inherent capacity to "lead on" (*opanayiko*) and hence no divine grace was found to be necessary. It was only a question of entering the Stream of Dhamma (*dhammasoto*) which runs counter (*paṭisotagāmī*) to the broader saṃsāric stream of suffering.

The realization here-and-now (*sandiṭṭhiko*) of the spiritual goal as represented by truth, light and deathlessness does not put the emancipated one totally out of alignment with the world, preventing all mediation. In the principle of Dependent Arising (see Ch. IV) he has discovered a safeguard against the conflicts that normally arise when there is an unbridgeable gap between levels of experience. The

---

83. Cf. *Kāyena amataṃ dhātuṃ phusayitvā nirūpadhiṃ / upadhipaṭinissaggaṃ sacchikatvā anāsavo / deseti sammāsambuddho asokaṃ virajaṃ padaṃ*—It IV 62

"Having touched with the body the Deathless Element which is Asset-less and realized the relinquishment of all assets, the Fully Enlightened One, who is influx-free, teaches the Sorrowless, Taintless State."

84. This state is also known as *ānantarika-samādhi*—"immediate concentration" (see Sn 226). The timeless (*akāliko*) nature of the Dhamma is implied here.

Kāḷakārāma Sutta in particular portrays how cautious the Buddha was in this concern. Nor is it the case that the realization of a transcendental sphere of experience has put his sense-faculties out of alignment (see fn. 10, p. 9), save for the fact that lust, hatred and delusion no longer affect their functioning. His synoptic understanding of the five aspects in regard to the six sense-spheres[85] enables him to live *in* the world though he is not *of* the world,[86] and it is in this respect that the "Nibbāna-element-with-residual-clinging" (*saupādisesa nibbānadhātu*) becomes significant.

"... And what, monks, is the Nibbāna-element-with-residual-clinging? Herein, monks, a monk is an arahant whose influxes are extinct, who has lived out the holy life, accomplished the task, laid down the burden, reached his goal, whose fetters of existence are fully extinct and who is freed through right knowledge. His five sense-faculties still remain, which being undestroyed, he partakes of the pleasant and the unpleasant and experiences the pleasurable and the painful. The extinction of lust, hatred and delusion in him—this, monks, is called the Nibbāna-element-with-residual-clinging"—It 38f.

Even though the emancipated one apparently "comes back" to the world of sense-experience, the bliss of Nibbāna is yet the same "inward-peace" (*ajjhattasanti*) or appeasement (*upasama*). Like other aspects of transcendence, this too is not always easily appreciated by the world. That there could be a form of bliss in the absence of desires, is something that is equally paradoxical as the ones cited before. And yet radical reflection might reveal that, as a matter of fact, it is not the desire that is blissful, but its appeasement. Desire, being a

---

85. "By the Tathāgata, monks, that incomparable excellent state of peace has been fully understood, that is to say, that deliverance without grasping, having understood as they really are the arising, the passing-away, the satisfaction, the misery and the "stepping-out" in regard to the six sense spheres"—M II 237, *Pañcattaya Sutta* (see also *Brahmajāla Sutta*).

form of stress and tension, like hunger and thirst, is in itself a malady, and it is only its "appeasement" that even in our "normal" life brings happiness. The tragedy, however, is that the appeasement bought at the price of the desired object is short-lived, for even like a fire desire flares up again with renewed force. It is owing to this fact that the Buddha did not recognize it as a real appeasement. On the contrary, he saw in it a vain attempt to extinguish a fire by adding more and more fuel to it. The principle underlying the attempt to appease desires nevertheless reveals that desires in themselves are not blissful. Now, if appeasement of desires is what is really blissful, "desirelessness" as the appeasement of all desires would be the Supreme Bliss and this in fact is what Nibbāna is.[87]

Unfortunately, the most widely known epithet for the *summum bonum* of Buddhism has acquired in course of time a stigma of being too negative in its connotations. Despite

---

86. Since his transcendence is final and complete, there is actually no "coming-back." "Once crossed over, the Such-like One comes not back" (*pāraṅgato na pacceti tādī*—Sn 803). Yet his alternation between the two Nibbāna-elements, *anupādisesa* (i.e., *nirūpadhiṃ*) and *saupādisesa*, is an apparent "return."

Na paraṃ diguṇaṃ yanti-na idaṁ ekaguṇaṃ mutaṃ
"They go not twice to the further shore
Nor yet is it reckoned a going-once"—Sn 714.

"Released, detached and delivered from ten things, Bāhuna, does the Tathāgata dwell with a mind unrestricted. Which are the ten? Released, detached and delivered from form does the Tathāgata dwell with a mind unrestricted. Released, detached and delivered from feeling, from perception, from formations, from consciousness, from birth, from decay, from death, from pains, from defilements, Bahuna, does the Tathāgata dwell with a mind unrestricted. Just as, Bāhuna, a blue, red or white lotus born in the water, grown in the water, comes up above the surface of the water and remains unsmeared with water, even so the Tathāgata—being released, detached and delivered from these ten things—dwells with a mind unrestricted"—A V 152.

obvious canonical evidence there is a hesitation to recognize the fact that it essentially signifies an extinguishing (if not "extinction"—the dismal word!). There is something traumatic in one's response to the so-called "negative definitions" and hence we usually leave the word "Nibbāna" untranslated, though its more "sociable" companions[88] fare better in this respect. This tendency becomes more marked when, for instance, Nibbāna is clearly defined in the Suttas as the "destruction of lust, hatred and delusion" and then even the commentary (S-a) is rather apologetic. If, as mentioned above, "desirelessness" is itself the Supreme Bliss, perhaps Nibbāna could easily vindicate its rights to be considered a "positive" happiness. Since the totality of existence is illustrated by the simile of the fire, Nibbāna as its extinction is also the experience of appeasement or tranquillity. It is, therefore, associated with the idea of becoming cool: "Having become hunger-less, extinguished, and grown cool even here and now, I proclaim Parinibbāna (perfect extinguishing) which is free from clinging (or fuel)."—A V 65. This "perfect extinguishing" or "appeasement" which involves no "fuel" at all is one that could be enjoyed "free-of-charge": "Those who, with a firm mind exert themselves well in the dispensation of Gotama, they being free from desire have reached their goal and having plunged into the Deathless (*amataṃ vigayha*), are enjoying the appeasement (*nibbuti*) obtained 'free-of-charge' (*mudha*) ..."—Sn 228, *Ratana Sutta*.

---

87. Nibbāna is the appeasement of all feelings as well, for, "Whatever is felt, is concerned with pain" (*yaṃ kiñci vedayitaṃ taṃ dukkhasmiṃ*"—S II 53).

When the venerable Sāriputta declared: "Friend, this Nibbāna is bliss! This Nibbāna is bliss!," the venerable Udāyi asked him: "What bliss is there, friend Sāriputta, where there is no feeling?" The reply was: "This itself, friend, is the bliss therein—the fact that there is no feeling" (A IV 414f.).

88. Thirty-three epithets are given at S IV 368ff.

With the appeasement of formations (*saṅkhārūpasama*) the "magic-show" of consciousness ends for the emancipated one, well before it ends as scheduled—at death. The magic has lost its magic for him and never again will he waste his "time" and "money" on such empty shows. Before he makes his "exit" he has gained an unshakable conviction (*aññā*) of the emptiness of the show, now that he has seen the wily tricks of the magician. Instead of the bliss-of-ignorance enjoyed by the frenzied worldly audience, he has enjoyed gratis the tranquil bliss-of-emancipation—the Supreme, Noble Appeasement (*paramo ariyo upasamo*—M III 246, *Dhātuvibhaṅga Sutta*). "There is no bliss higher than peace" (*natthi santiparaṃ sukhaṃ*—Dhp 202).

Through many a saṃsāric birth I ran
Seeking the house-builder in vain
Pain it is to be born again and again
O! house-builder, thou art seen
Thou shalt build no house again
Shattered lie all thy rafters
Thy roof-top is torn asunder
Mind attained cankerless state
Reached is cravings' end.

Dhp 153–4

THE BUDDHIST PUBLICATION SOCIETY

The BPS is an approved charity dedicated to making known the Teaching of the Buddha, which has a vital message for all people.

Founded in 1958, the BPS has published a wide variety of books and booklets covering a great range of topics. Its publications include accurate annotated translations of the Buddha's discourses, standard reference works, as well as original contemporary expositions of Buddhist thought and practice. These works present Buddhism as it truly is—a dynamic force which has influenced receptive minds for the past 2500 years and is still as relevant today as it was when it first arose.

For more information about the BPS and our publications, please visit our website, or write an e-mail or letter to:

The Administrative Secretary
Buddhist Publication Society
P.O. Box 61
54 Sangharaja Mawatha
Kandy • Sri Lanka

E-mail: bps@sltnet.lk
web site: http://www.bps.lk
Tel: 0094 81 223 7283 • Fax: 0094 81 222 3679